THE GENUS
LEWISIA

A KEW MAGAZINE MONOGRAPH

The Genus
LEWISIA

Brian Mathew

Illustrations by
Christabel King

Series Editors
Christopher Grey-Wilson
Victoria Matthews

The Royal Botanic Gardens, Kew
in association with Christopher Helm
and Timber Press

Copyright © Bentham-Moxon Trust, Royal Botanic Gardens, Kew, 1989

Christopher Helm (Publishers) Ltd, Imperial House,
21–25 North Street, Bromley, Kent BR1 1SD

ISBN 0-7470-2217-8

First published in North America
in 1989 by
Timber Press Inc.
9999 S.W. Wilshire
Portland, Oregon 97225

ISBN 0-88192-158-0

Typeset by Paston Press, Loddon, Norfolk
Printed and bound in Great Britain by Butler and Tanner, Frome, Somerset

CONTENTS

LIST OF COLOUR PLATES

ACKNOWLEDGEMENTS

Many people have generously imparted their knowledge of lewisias and it is difficult to say which have contributed the most, for sometimes just one small piece of information has been extremely important. In particular, however, I must offer my greatest thanks to Roy Davidson, Sean Hogan, Janet Hohn, Wayne Roderick, Sally and Tim Walker and Margaret Williams for supplying me with so much invaluable information about lewisias in the wild, either by personal contact or through their writings. Kath Dryden V.M.H. (who has written the cultivation chapter and provided many of the plants illustrated in the colour plates), Roy Elliott (author of the only *Lewisia* monograph to have been published), Philip Baulk of Ashwood Nurseries, Brian Halliwell and Tony Hall of the Royal Botanic Gardens, Kew, all gave a great deal of help concerning lewisias in cultivation, and I must also not forget Joy Bishop who kindly sacrificed some plants of rare species in the interests of research, and Margaret Johnson of Kew who cut them up and provided chromosome counts.

The artwork has been prepared by Christabel King and I am grateful to her for enhancing the book with her beautiful illustrations. Thanks are also due to Brinsley Burbidge, Michael Ireland, Wayne Roderick and Tim Walker for supplying some of the colour photographs of lewisias, both in their wild state and in cultivation.

I must also say to the Editors of the Kew Magazine Monograph series, Christopher Grey-Wilson and Victoria Matthews, that I am grateful for their assistance and for the remarkable restraint they showed as manuscript deadlines passed by!

Finally, this is a suitable place to record that my enthusiasm for the genus is derived directly from that of Mr A.G. Weeks, one of the early *Lewisia* breeders, in whose garden I had the pleasure of working during the summer of 1957.

INTRODUCTION

The genus *Lewisia* is restricted to western North America. It comprises some 19 species which exhibit a range of leaf form and flower size and colour. The larger-flowered species such as *L. cotyledon*, *L. rediviva* and *L. tweedyi* are exquisite in full flower, but most lewisias, even those with small flowers, have a great deal of charm. The lewisias with large flowers are the ones best known to the gardening public, indeed *L. rediviva* and cultivars of *L. cotyledon* are sometimes offered by garden centres. *Lewisia cotyledon*, whose flowers, usually with striped petals, show a remarkable range of colour from white, through shades of pink, apricot, salmon, yellow and orange to red, is one of the most spectacular of all alpines when in full flower; its potential as a pot-plant is now being investigated in the Netherlands and other countries.

This is the first major published revision of the genus since 1966. The last few years have seen an increase in popularity of lewisias, particularly with those gardeners who specialize in alpines and who have alpine houses and frames where the environment can be controlled. Genera such as *Lewisia* offer a challenge to the keen gardener. However, not all the species are difficult to grow and several, especially *L. cotyledon* and *L. columbiana*, can be grown out-of-doors, provided that the conditions are right.

All but one of the species hybridize fairly readily and thus offer the enterprising gardener plenty of scope for producing hybrids and selecting the better forms.

In this book the main concern is with the species, although hybrids and cultivars of garden origin are also included. Some species have a wide distribution, whereas others are extremely local. At the present time lewisias are not endangered in the wild, but fashions in plants can change rapidly and a sudden increase in demand, resulting in large-scale collecting, could quickly deplete populations of the rarer species. Collection of wild plants is quite unnecessary as the species of lewisia can be raised from seed. Whereas judicious collection of wild seed is acceptable, wholesale removal of plants from wild habitats can only be condemned.

Brian Mathew is well known for his books on bulbous plants and his monographs of *Iris* and *Crocus*. *Hellebores*, his most recent book, was recently published by the Alpine Garden Society. The present monograph on *Lewisia* is the result of several years' research.

The beautiful watercolours by Christabel King have been prepared from living plants, mainly supplied from the collections of the Royal Botanic Gardens, Kew and by Mrs Kath Dryden whose knowledge and experience of lewisia cultivation is a great asset to this book.

Christopher Grey-Wilson
Victoria Matthews

HISTORY AND
RELATIONSHIPS OF THE
GENUS

The genus *Lewisia* was described by Frederick Pursh in his *Flora Americae Septentrionalis* 2: 368 (1814), based on a specimen collected by Captain Meriwether Lewis during the Lewis and Clark expedition the aim of which was to cross from the eastern States to the Pacific by way of the Missouri and Columbia rivers. It was one of a 'small but highly interesting collection of dried plants' consisting of about 150 specimens which Pursh noted as containing not more than 'a dozen plants well known to me to be natives of North America, the rest being either entirely new or but little known, and among them at least six distinct and new genera'. The story of how Lewis's dried specimen was subsequently removed from the herbarium and brought into growth again is told later on in this book under the description of the species, but is mentioned here to explain Pursh's choice of the epithet *rediviva* for the type species of his new genus.

There has never been any real doubt that *Lewisia* belongs in the family Portulacaceae A.L. de Jussieu (1789) although Lewisiaceae Hooker & Arnott made a brief appearance in 1839. The relationships at the family level, however, do receive varied treatments. Bentham & Hooker (1862) associated the Portulacaceae with the larger family Caryophyllaceae, but others have expressed the view that perhaps the Cactaceae should be considered as a near relative, and one has to admit when looking at some of the lewisias, notably *L. rediviva*, that this idea has certain attractions. In Engler's *Syllabus der Pflanzenfamilien* (ed. 12, 1964) the Portulacaceae, Caryophyllaceae, and several other families, are placed together in the order Centrospermae and this is in fact situated adjacent to the order Cactales in this particular system of classification. J. Hutchinson (1973), however, considered that the family, and *Lewisia* in particular, might in some evolutionary way be connected with the Primulaceae and noted that it 'is a highly interesting family, for in the structure of its flowers it seems to point very clearly to the evolution of the more advanced Primulaceae . . . in *Lewisia* the

11

capsule dehisces by a circumscissile slit as in the Primulaceous genera *Soldanella*, *Bryocarpus*, *Anagallis* and *Centrunculus*'.

McNeill (1974) regards the Portulacaceae as comprising between 15 and 30 genera with 500 species. The subgeneric classification by Pax & Hoffmann (1934) is considered to be unsatisfactory by McNeill and the proposed revised system is based at least in part on the earlier work by Fenzl (1836, 1839) but also takes into account recent surveys by several other workers. The 1974 classification divides the family into seven tribes, one of which is tribe III *Lewisieae* Torrey & A. Gray ex Walpers, *Repertorium Botanices Systematicae* 5: 790 (1846), in which *Lewisia* is the only genus.

Generically, *Lewisia* is best defined largely by its fruiting characters. Of all the genera in the Portulacaceae only *Portulaca* L., *Calyptrotheca* Gilg and *Lewisia* Pursh have circumscissile capsules; the other genera, including the North American *Calandrinia* Kunth, *Claytonia* L., *Montia* L. and *Talinum* Adans., have valvate or indehiscent capsules. *Calyptrotheca*, although having circumscissile fruits, is far removed from *Lewisia* in its other features and consists of two shrubby species from Africa. *Talinum* is very distinct from *Lewisia* in that is has a semi-inferior ovary, and the 'cap' of the fruit separates off towards the apex; in *Lewisia* the line of dehiscence is towards the base of the capsule and the ovary is superior. *Lewisia* and *Calandrinia* have probably been the most frequently confused of the American genera and the Central American species of *Calandrinia* have by some authors been considered to be congeneric with the North American lewisias. However, it has been shown that apart from the distinguishing capsule features there are important and consistent pollen differences, so it is clear that the two genera should be considered as distinct. *Lewisia* is therefore an entirely North American genus, not reaching as far south as Mexico whereas *Calandrinia* is predominantly South American, extending northwards into Mexico. Thus, *L. megarhiza* (Hemsley) MacBryde (syn. *Calandrinia megarhiza*, *Claytonia megarhiza*, *Oreobroma megarhizum*), which occurs in Guatemala and Mexico, is better placed in *Calandrinia* (Kelley & Swanson, 1985), which is where it began its nomenclatural wanderings in 1897 when first described by Hemsley.

Most of the species of *Lewisia*, as currently recognized, have in the past been described in, or transferred to, other genera. *Oreobroma* was described by Thomas Howell in 1893 to encompass all the then known *Lewisia* species, except for the type species *L. rediviva*. The diagnostic features for this genus were the possession of only two sepals (six to eight in *L. rediviva*) and correspondingly fewer petals and stamens; also considered to be significant was the jointed stem in *L. rediviva*, which allowed the whole flower to break off in the fruiting stage for dispersal purposes. *Erocallis* Rydberg was a monotypic genus erected in 1906 for the somewhat unusual *L. triphylla* which possesses a nearly globose corm, lacks any basal leaves at flowering time and has whorled leaves borne on the stem. Neither of these genera, however, is considered to be worthy of recognition and all the species concerned are here retained in *Lewisia*.

HISTORY OF LEWISIAS IN CULTIVATION

Lewisias as cultivated plants are relatively recent in terms of garden history, the earliest to arrive in Britain, during the second half of the nineteenth century, being *L. rediviva*, *L. brachycalyx*, *L. nevadensis*, *L. oppositifolia* and *L. tweedyi*. No selection or hybridization appears to have taken place in these early days and these seem to have been mostly 'one-off' introductions to establishments such as Kew Gardens. The dates of introduction into cultivation do of course bear a close relationship to the dates when the newly discovered species were given their first formal botanical names and descriptions; a chronological list of these dates appears in Appendix 2 (p. 140).

The genus did not really gain any marked popularity until the showy and relatively easily cultivated *L. cotyledon* was introduced, probably at about the turn of the century. This was described in 1885 and had certainly reached Kew by 1906, and the related *L. columbiana* arrived at about the same time. However, it seems that it was not until the 1930s that there were any serious moves to develop lewisias, and this was at the time when the Alpine Garden Society was in an active state of evolution. The name of F. W. Millard, of Camla, Felbridge, near East Grinstead, West Sussex, figures prominently in the early days of *Lewisia* cultivation, and it is reported (*Journal of the Royal Horticultural Society* 60: 159, 1935) that he received his first *Lewisia* in the spring of 1913 (*L. cotyledon* var. *howellii*). In an account of his garden (*Bulletin Alpine Garden Society* 2: 9, 1933) it was noted that lewisias were a particular speciality of Millard's and that he grew *L. howellii*, *L. cotyledon*, *L. purdyi*, *L. heckneri*, *L. columbiana*, *L. columbiana* 'Rosea', *L. leeana*, *L. pygmaea* and *L. tweedyi*. The last was said to form great 'cabbages' wherever it was planted! The first lewisia plants which he received are reputed to have been sent to him by Mary L. White of Waldo, southern Oregon (after whom *L.* × *whiteae* is named), whose husband Homer was a stage-coach driver on the Oregon to California road (Rowntree, 1972). Millard found that his lewisias, 'when brought into association hybridize shamelessly, and it is almost impossible under such circumstances to keep

14

any variety true'. By 1935 he was obviously fairly well advanced in the selection of lewisias for he remarked that he had 'succeeded in obtaining deep rich carmine, lovely pinks, and several intermediate shades, and, strange to say, many are self coloured, all signs of the stripe having been eliminated'. In 1942 Millard exhibited a fine range of lewisias, as 'Millard's Hybrids', at a Royal Horticultural Society show on 19 May. F.W. Millard was, however, not the only enthusiast for the genus and in the RHS article cited above he mentions Mr Walpole, of Mt. Usher, Co. Wicklow, as being one of the pioneers of *Lewisia* growing. The Royal Horticultural Society's garden at Wisley also cultivated them and in 1935 had *L. finchae*, *L. heckneri* and *L. cotyledon*, as well as numerous hybrids said to be more beautiful than their parents.

Mr A.G. Weeks of Weald Cottage, Limpsfield Chart, Surrey was also one of the earlier growers and raisers of new lewisias and was responsible for some good cultivars such as 'Weald Rose' and 'Rose Splendour'. Writing in the *Journal of the Royal Horticultural Society* for 1959, Mr Weeks stated that he had grown *L. howellii* for 20 years and that after a few years a pale pink seedling had appeared; then in 1948 a beautiful rose-coloured form arose and this received an Award of Merit in 1951 as 'Weald Rose'. Subsequently he saved seed from that plant and obtained a range of colours varying from deep rose to orange and pale yellow. He exhibited at the Chelsea Show in 1958 and was also awarded a Silver Medal for a 'wonderful collection of Lewisias' at the 3rd International Rock Garden Conference on 18 April 1961.

The East Grinstead alpine nursery of Messrs W. E. Th. Ingwersen was in close contact with both A. G. Weeks and F. W. Millard and certainly received plants, including 'Weald Rose' and 'Rose Splendour', during the 1950s when I was gaining some work experience at the nursery, following on from a period of assisting Mr Weeks at Weald Cottage. Messrs Ingwersen continued the process of selection in the *L. cotyledon* group and raised some good cultivars of their own including the excellent 'George Henley' (a *L. cotyledon* × *L. columbiana* hybrid probably with the latter as seed parent), and a variable strain called 'Birch Hybrids'. Later, the dwarf 'Pinkie' arose at the nursery, clearly the result of a cross between *L. cotyledon* and what was known at the time as '*L. pygmaea* of gardens', now known to be *L. longipetala*.

Joe Elliott of Broadwell Nursery, Moreton-in-Marsh,

15

Gloucestershire, was also actively hybridizing various species in the 1950s and 1960s and obtained, among others, the very good dwarf *L.* 'Phyllellia' (*L. brachycalyx* × *L. cotyledon*) which is still to be found in cultivation. In Scotland, Jack Drake's Inshriach Nursery at Aviemore worked on a remarkably vivid race of *L. cotyledon* selections which was subsequently called the 'Sunset Strain' and which is now being produced by the thousand and is extremely popular.

Before 1966 there was no monograph of the genus *Lewisia* but in that year an excellent 'gardeners' guide' was produced by R. C. Elliott for the Alpine Garden Society. In acquiring data for this book a great number of lewisia plants were gathered together and, at a London show on 25 April 1967, Roy Elliott exhibited 13 species and their colour variants and hundreds of garden hybrids, a remarkable collection. The publication of this book, and its reprint in 1978, undoubtedly largely accounts for the great popularity of the genus at the present time. The process of cultivation, hybridization and selection continues and, although it is impossible to review the work of all those who are involved, I should mention at least some of the main growers. Mrs Kath Dryden exhibited a remarkable collection of 14 species and a very full colour range of *L. cotyledon* hybrids at the Chelsea Show in 1983 and received a Gold Lindley Medal. Mrs Joy Bishop expertly cultivates many of the species, and Philip Baulk, of Ashwood Nurseries, Kingswinford, has a good range of species and is raising some excellent cultivars including a good yellow *L. cotyledon* strain. Potterton and Martin, of The Cottage Nursery, Nettleton, Lincolnshire, are also raising and selecting a considerable number. In the United States, J. Cobb Colley and Baldassare Mineo, the proprietors of the Siskiyou Rare Plant Nursery and authors of a beautifully illustrated article in *Pacific Horticulture* (summer 1985), and Phil Pearson and Steve Doonan of Grand Ridge Nursery in Washington State, also have good collections.

All of these people are or have been involved with lewisias, either in the development of an enhanced range of cultivars or in the maintenance and propagation of these lovely plants for others to enjoy, but one must also not forget the field work carried out by those who have collected seeds in the wild and distributed them. For example, Charles Thurman, of Spokane, Washington, sent seeds of *L. tweedyi* to Britain and these gave rise to variably coloured plants including a pure white which was raised by Jack Drake of Inshriach Nursery and named 'Alba'. Carl Purdy in the late nineteenth century and early years of this century was responsible for collecting and introducing many lewisias, via his nursery, some of which he described as new species, such as *L. whiteae*, *L. finchae* and *L. eastwoodiana*; he did unfortunately collect large quantities of *L. cotyledon* for direct sale from the wild and may have been responsible for reducing some populations to unacceptably low levels. In recent years Wayne Roderick and Margaret Williams have supplied seeds of many unusual species to *Lewisia* enthusiasts and have freely given their invaluable field knowledge to growers to assist in the tricky task of trying to cultivate them.

MORPHOLOGY

Lewisias are glabrous succulent perennial herbs of low-growing habit with fleshy root-stocks which allow the plants to withstand long periods of summer drought. There are both evergreen and deciduous species.

THE ROOT-STOCK AND CAUDEX

In most species the underground parts of the plant consist of a thick, fleshy taproot which is usually branched and is provided with extremely fine secondary roots. The upper part of the taproot, which is often fusiform, is positioned near the soil surface and the leaves are produced from the apex, usually in a loose tuft or dense rosette. As the plant matures a short thick stem or 'caudex' is produced which may be clothed in its lower parts with the older shrivelled leaves. This caudex may be simple or branched so that there are several 'heads' of leaf-rosettes per plant; with age it may develop so that it is well above ground level. An exception to these generalizations is *L. triphylla* which has a small, almost spherical tuber and no caudex.

THE LEAVES

The foliage of lewisias is very fleshy, although in the case of *L. congdonii* the leaves are fairly thin compared with those of most species. Some (species 14–19) have evergreen rosettes while others (species 1–13) are deciduous, and in the latter category the majority are summer-deciduous, dying down at the onset of the dry summer months; a few are winter-deciduous. Most species are nearly stemless (except for the short thick caudex) and have the leaves densely arranged in basal tufts or symmetrical rosettes, but in *L. oppositifolia* they are arranged in pairs on a fairly well-developed aerial stem, while *L. triphylla* produces them in whorls of three.

The leaf shape ranges from very narrowly linear and more or less cylindrical to spatulate, oblanceolate or narrowly obovate. In many species the lower part of the leaf, instead of narrowing to a distinct petiole, is widened with wing-like papery margins. The leaf-margin is smooth in most species but toothed in *L. cantelovii*, some variants of *L. cotyledon* and in *L. serrata*, and the apex may be acute, obtuse or rounded.

THE INFLORESCENCE

There is a wide range of inflorescence type in *Lewisia*. Most species produce their flowers in cymes or in panicles but a few, such as *L. rediviva* and *L. nevadensis*, have solitary flowers; *L. triphylla* may have subumbellate inflorescences, and in *L. oppositifolia* the few flowers may be arranged in an almost corymbose manner. In some cases the inflorescence is more or less racemose, as in *L. tweedyi*. The bracts are entire or glandular-toothed and are arranged alternately, oppositely or in whorls; in some species the lowest ones may be leaf-like, decreasing in size upwards, but the upper bracts subtending the flowers are always much reduced. There are considerable differences between the bracts of the various species; *L. cotyledon*, for example, has alternate, glandular-toothed bracts, in *L. nevadensis* they are paired, smooth and green, while in *L. rediviva* there are up to 10 subulate or linear-lanceolate papery bracts in a whorl.

In most species the flowers are pedicellate, i.e., there is a stalk between the bract or bracts and the flower. However, in two species, *L. brachycalyx* and *L. kelloggii*, there is no pedicel and the two bracts are situated immediately adjacent to the two sepals so that at first it appears that there are four sepals to each flower.

THE FLOWER

The *Lewisia* flower is usually large and showy, and often exhibits the brilliant pink and magenta colours associated with the Portulacaceae, although there are several white-flowered species. The perianth has two whorls. The outer whorl is a calyx consisting, in most species, of two small opaque green or purplish sepals, but *L. rediviva* and *L. maguirei* have three or more large 'petaloid' sepals which are papery and white or pinkish. The inner whorl consists of several larger, showier, thin-textured petals which vary considerably and inconsistently in number; most species have between five and nine petals but *L. rediviva* has up to 19, making it one of the showiest, with a flower diameter of 5–6 cm whereas in *L. sierrae* the flower diameter is only about 1 cm. Within one flower the petals are seldom exactly the same size, especially in width. Usually the petal-margins are entire but sometimes there are teeth at the apex and occasionally the teeth are glandular as, for example, in *L. pygmaea*. After anthesis the corolla shrivels and twists somewhat so that it encloses the stamens, style and ovary, and does not usually fall off until the capsule is fairly well developed. J. Hohn (1975), however, notes that in *L. tweedyi* the corolla falls soon after pollination so that the developing capsule is exposed early.

THE STAMENS AND POLLEN

The number of stamens in *Lewisia* flowers varies widely between the species and even within a species; there may be as few as five to nine in *L. cotyledon*, for example, and between 20 and 50 in *L. rediviva*. They have versatile anthers and filiform filaments which are capable of movement, arching outwards away from their initial erect posture until they are positioned well away from the stigmas, presumably a mechanism designed to promote cross-pollination rather than self-pollination.

A thorough survey of *Lewisia* pollen is required in order to ascertain whether features such as the surface architecture and the structure of the grains are of any value taxonomically. J. Hohn (1975) made a palynological study of *L. cotyledon* and its allies, and *L. tweedyi*, and found that there was a marked degree of similarity between them all in this respect but that *L. tweedyi* differed slightly from the rest; it is possible, therefore, that pollen data might help in assessing the relationship between the various subgenera and sections of the genus.

THE OVARY AND STYLE

The ovary varies somewhat in shape from almost globose to ovoid or subcylindrical, or sometimes slightly three-cornered longitudinally. In some species there are rather few ovules, such as *L. leeana* with only two to four, while others, for instance *L. rediviva* and *L. tweedyi*, may have up to 25 or more. The single slender style is divided to varying degrees in its upper part into three to eight branches which are erect at first but soon spread apart widely.

THE FRUIT AND SEED

The *Lewisia* fruit is a thin-walled capsule which is circumscissile near its base, thus allowing the whole upper portion to fall off like a cap; there is also a tendency for the capsule walls to split lengthways but the initial line of dehiscence is certainly horizontal. The removal of the 'cap' reveals the seeds which are then free to be distributed. In most species this is effected quite simply by the seeds falling out if slightly disturbed, but the seeds of *L. tweedyi*, which have a fleshy appendage (strophiole), are probably distributed by ants. *Lewisia rediviva*, *L. maguirei* and *L. disepala* differ in that there is a joint at the base of the pedicel which breaks, allowing the dried flower(s) together with the capsule to fall and to be dispersed by the wind; the large papery sepals assist in this process.

J. Hohn (1975) has studied the capsule of *L. tweedyi* and reports that its method of dehiscence differs from that of *L. cotyledon* and its allies, and, it appears, from that of most other species as well. The capsule 'dehisces apically along 3 to 6 valves and secondarily becomes loosened at the base, eventually dropping off in sections. Unlike the scapes of related species which remain erect, the peduncles in *L. tweedyi* undergo a post-pollination curvature of near 180°, positioning the developing capsule near the base of the plant in an inverted position.' This presumably helps in the distribution of the seeds by ants.

The seeds are ovoid to reniform or suborbicular, usually black and glossy, but sometimes dark brown, minutely tuberculate (prominently so in *L. tweedyi*), and with or without a fleshy appendage or strophiole (only present in *L. tweedyi*). J. Hohn (1975) in her study of *L. cotyledon* and its allies (in which *L. tweedyi* was included) noted that 'subtle interspecific differences in testa, size of the seed, and shape of the embryo, comprise important taxonomic characters'. This suggests that a detailed seed survey of the whole genus might be of some value but it would be necessary to sample wild populations rather than cultivated material; this would be a considerable task in the case of the widespread species such as *L. triphylla*, *L. pygmaea* and *L. rediviva*.

21

POLLINATION AND COMPATIBILITY

Little detailed information concerning pollination of lewisias is available but it is clear that they are pollinated mainly if not wholly by insects which utilize the nectar which is secreted around the base of the ovary and filaments. J. Hohn (1975) studied populations of *L. leeana* and *L. cotyledon* and recorded hover-flies and balloon-flies (Syrphidae and Acroceridae) and bees (*Adrena*, *Bombus*) actively engaged in visiting *Lewisia* flowers and, in doing so, becoming dusted with pollen; presumably their activities resulted in cross-pollination. Under cultivated conditions in Britain, bees are attracted to lewisias and, if a controlled hybridization programme is to be effective, steps must be taken to exclude them.

J. Hohn has shown quite convincingly that *L. cotyledon* and allied species are self-compatible and that at least some of the seeds produced are the result of insects transferring pollen from one flower to another on the same inflorescence. However, cross-pollination is encouraged because *Lewisia* flowers are protandrous, that is the stamens reach maturity before the stigmas, and they then arch outwards away from the stigmas to prevent self-pollination. This does not guarantee out-crossing, however, since pollen may still be successfully transferred between the flowers on one particular plant, but it does assist in the process.

CYTOLOGY

There has been, unfortunately, no thorough cytological investigation of the genus *Lewisia*, although chromosome counts are now available, from a number of different sources, for several of the species.

Prior to 1966 only two counts of chromosome numbers had been published, for *L. tweedyi* and *L. pygmaea*; then R. C. Elliott (1966) listed several counts which had been prepared at the Royal Botanic Gardens, Kew, by Mr M. Daker, but although valuable most of these were based on cultivated material of no known origin. The first real progress in this field was made by Dr Janet E. Hohn (1975) whose detailed studies concerned *L. cotyledon* and its allies and were based solely on wild source specimens. In 1986, Margaret Johnson of the Royal Botanic Gardens, Kew, added a few more counts and confirmed some of the previously reported chromosome numbers.

J. Hohn's observations were made using flower-buds taken from 'barely emergent inflorescences' to provide squashes of pollen mother cells, whereas most other chromosome counts have been made from squashes of actively growing root-tips. It appears that the former method gives the best results but is really only suitable for those species which produce fairly long inflorescences containing many flowers, such as *L. cotyledon*, *L. columbiana*, etc.; in these species the very young buds are fairly readily accessible. In the case of the very dwarf species, which mostly have rather few flowers on very short stems, it might be physically very difficult to obtain premature buds which contain pollen in its early stages of formation. Root-tip squashes in *Lewisia* provide less clearly visible results and it was found by Margaret Johnson at Kew (pers. comm.) that it was very difficult to see and count the chromosomes accurately; this was also noted by J. Hohn who commented that material 'prepared in this way did not result in any countable figures'.

The currently available diploid chromosome numbers are listed below, in the sequence of the species as published in the main body of the text of this book. The authority for the chromosome count is given in brackets, followed by the source of the material, if known.

1. *L. rediviva*	$2n = 28$ (M. Johnson, Kew) Canada, British Columbia, *B. Halliwell* 3826
2. *L. maguirei*	no chromosome count traced
3. *L. disepala*	no chromosome count traced
4. *L. kelloggii*	no chromosome count traced
5. *L. brachycalyx*	$2n = 20$ (M. Daker in Elliott, 1966). Cultivated stock, Royal Botanic Gardens, Kew
6. *L. triphylla*	no chromosome count traced
7. *L. oppositifolia*	no chromosome count traced
8. *L. nevadensis*	$2n = c. 56$ (M. Johnson, Kew). Cultivated stock, Royal Botanic Gardens, Kew
9. *L. longipetala*	no chromosome count traced
10. *L. sierrae*	no chromosome count traced
11. *L. pygmaea*	$2n = c. 66$ (D. Wiens & D.K. Halleck, 1962). Colorado, Boulder Co., *D. Wiens* 2862
12. *L. stebbinsii*	no chromosome count traced
13. *L. congdonii*	$2n = c. 24$ (M. Johnson, Kew). California; seeds sent to Royal Botanic Gardens, Kew by *W. Roderick*
14. *L. columbiana*	
subsp. *columbiana*	$2n = 30$ (J. Hohn, 1975). Washington, Okanagan Co., *J. Hohn* 1380
	$2n = 30$ (J. Hohn, 1975). Washington, Kittitas Co., *J. Hohn* 1353
subsp. *rupicola*	$2n = 30$ (J. Hohn, 1975). Washington, Jefferson Co., *J. Hohn* 1424

15. *L. leeana*	2n = 28 (M. Johnson, Kew). California, Castle Lake, Siskiyou Co., *B. Halliwell* 3079
	2n = 28 (J. Hohn, 1975). California, Trinity Co., *J. Hohn* 1134
16. *L. cantelovii*	2n = 28 (J. Hohn, 1975). California, Plumas Co., *J. Hohn* 1015
17. *L. serrata*	no chromosome count traced
18. *L. cotyledon*	
var. *cotyledon*	2n = 28 (J. Hohn, 1975). California, Siskiyou Co., *J. Hohn* 1225
	2n = 28 (M. Johnson, Kew). Cultivated stock, Royal Botanic Gardens, Kew
var. *howellii*	2n = 28 (J. Hohn, 1975). California, Siskiyou Co., *J. Hohn* 1231
	2n = 28 (J. Hohn, 1975). Oregon, Douglas Co., *J. Hohn* 1313
	2n = 28 (M. Johnson, Kew). Cultivated stock, Royal Botanic Gardens, Kew
var. *heckneri*	2n = 28 (J. Hohn, 1975). California, Trinity Co., *J. Hohn* 447
19. *L. tweedyi*	2n = 92 (Kruckeberg, 1957). Washington, Wenatchee Mts., *A. R. Kruckeberg* 3320
	2n = 92 (J. Hohn, 1975). Washington, Chelan Co., *J. Hohn* 1460
	2n = *c*. 92–95 (M. Daker in Elliott, 1966). Cultivated stock, Royal Botanic Gardens, Kew

In addition, the cultivar *L.* 'Trevosia' (*L. columbiana* × *L. cotyledon*) was studied at Kew and found to have a diploid number of 'about 28'. J. Hohn (1975) published counts of 2n = 28 for three *L. cotyledon* × *L. leeana* hybrids collected in California, Siskiyou County (*J. Hohn* 457, 506 and 1288).

CONSERVATION

Some of the *Lewisia* species are rather local endemics, and may even be considered to be rare, but information supplied to me by Christine Leon of the World Conservation Monitoring Centre at Kew suggests that at present none of the species is under threat; having said that it should be pointed out that for most of the species there is little information available on their conservation status. However, although they are apparently not in any great immediate danger, there is no excuse for digging up *Lewisia* plants on a large scale, even in the case of the relatively common and widespread species. It may of course be desirable occasionally to collect individual plants of horticulturally interesting variants, but for most purposes seed collection is an adequate and much more satisfactory way of introducing material into cultivation.

CULTIVATION

Lewisias have always carried the stigma of being considered particularly difficult to grow. This is, however, not the case providing one learns the precise requirements of each species and disciplines oneself to the routine care which they demand. It is, in reality, impossible to emulate their natural growing conditions exactly, but a knowledge of the climate and soil structure is essential, as is knowledge of when and how plants rest in the wild.

Unfortunately, the botanical groupings are of little help in choosing appropriate cultivation methods; neither is it possible to make cultural distinction between the evergreen and deciduous types.

A collection of *Lewisia* species in pots can be grown in a standard glasshouse which is provided with extra ventilation and a door at each end. In winter the vents are closed but the doors remain open as much as possible—all day except when frosts persist. A fan heater is set to switch on at 1°C—this is enough to prevent the pots from becoming frozen, though not enough to keep frost out of the house.

Lewisias undoubtedly grow best in clay pots, which should be plunged in sand throughout the year; only the plunge material should be watered. They can, however, be watered copiously during the spring and also once or twice in the autumn. Providing the plants are repotted regularly, feeding is not necessary—in any event only fertilizers which are low in nitrogen should be used. *Lewisia cotyledon* hybrids will grow reasonably well in plastic pots and can be overwintered in very severe conditions in cold frames, but they rarely make long-lived plants under these conditions. Grown slowly in good clay pots the first three years are critical, but if they come through this period they will often live for up to 20 years; the gradual loss of flowers is a good indication that the plant is nearing the completion of its life span.

OUTDOOR CULTIVATION

Remarkable *Lewisia* specimens can be seen in a number of gardens growing in troughs outdoors or on north facing screes on 45° slopes. There is a famous vertical wall at Bodnant in North Wales where *L. cotyledon* hybrids flourish, but it is exceptional to see them growing this well. Providing that one is prepared to experiment, and risk many losses, it can be fun to try them in the open garden, but for the best chance of success they should always be planted on a slope (north to north-west facing is ideal). In such positions they will take a considerable amount of rain, providing the drainage is good around the neck. However, in hot weather they detest being watered with a hose and it is best to cover them while the other plants are being watered. If they become very dry the plants will fold their leaves over the centre, and 'sleep' until autumn, just as they do in the wild.

The deciduous species such as *L. oppositifolia* and *L. pygmaea* are not at all easy to grow outside, and many people find they are difficult in a bulb frame. As a result they are most often seen cossetted in the close confines of the alpine house.

GROWING FROM SEED

The vast majority of lewisias are grown from seed, either home-saved or in tiny quantities from wild collections. The seed is sown in autumn whenever possible, sowing very thinly on the surface of a 50:50 peat and gritty sand mixture and covered with sharp grit. The pots are then left out to the vagaries of the weather. They can stand temperatures as low as −5°C, but freezing for long periods once the seed is wet can kill them. Seed sown after the new year normally takes a year to germinate, whereas germination of autumn-sown seed often takes place during the succeeding winter. When this occurs the pots should be taken into the alpine house, since the freeze-thaw action lifts the small root-system and inhibits growth.

All of the evergreen species can be pricked out as soon as they are large enough to handle, but the deciduous types are best left in their pots until their second autumn. The young plants should be given weak feeds during their second year of growth, with a well-balanced fertilizer.

COMPOSTS

For simplicity, with four exceptions (*L. cotyledon*, *L. columbiana*, *L. rediviva* and *L. tweedyi*), lewisias can all be grown in the same compost, i.e. 1 part John Innes potting compost No. 3, 1 part peat and 1 part grit (see also individual cultivation requirements, below). For those who cannot obtain John Innes composts a suitable alternative would be 2 parts peat and 1½ parts grit, plus a good slow-release fertilizer, used as instructed by the manufacturers.

POTTING

The vast majority of lewisias which are cultivated in gardens are in the *L. cotyledon* group. The young plants should be pricked out into 5 cm pots, potted on three times during their first season and kept moist and shaded. By the end of the following winter the young plants will be ready for 13 cm pots—it is wise to choose wide rather than deep pots to allow the roots to spread out horizontally. If the young plants are left underpotted they will flower prematurely and usually they will die as a result. This is unfortunately common nursery practice, although some growers now offer good plants grown on into 1 litre pots that will, with care, live for as many as 20 years—those will of course cost more.

In succeeding years the plants should be completely repotted—all the soil is shaken or washed off and, if possible, the plants repotted in similar sized pots in fresh compost. Repotting can be tackled any time from autumn to late winter. The soil should be hand-damp and no further water given until it is evident that new growth is under way in the centre of the leaf-rosette. Repotting in summer is very tricky and the plants must be kept densely shaded and in active growth. If they dry out at this stage they will become dormant and it is difficult to revive them in autumn in the new loose compost.

In the autumn there will be a natural withering of leaves from the outside of the rosette. They should not be tidied up but allowed to wither back untouched—this applies to *all* lewisias. If the dying leaves are ripped off there will be an undesirable proliferation of offsets. Ideally, plants are seen at their best with a single large rosette, but if more are required leave not more than three or four well-spaced peripheral offsets, having rubbed off unwanted ones

29

while they were very young. A huge overcrowded dome may have 'flower power' but such plants are completely out of character.

VEGETATIVE PROPAGATION

Any lewisia that makes sideshoots or offshoots can be increased vegetatively. This is best carried out in spring before flowering, indeed this timing is imperative with the deciduous types. In the case of interspecific hybrids this is the only way of increasing them since they are all, so far as it is known, infertile. Occasionally a few seeds are produced but so far none has been known to germinate. The offsets should be cut off cleanly close to the caudex using a sharp knife. They should then be inserted in sand and kept in a close atmosphere for a few weeks. However, increasing *L. tweedyi* from offsets can be frustrating as they frequently collapse and die when apparently quite healthy. *Lewisia rediviva* can be increased vegetatively with much more time and patience; the growing point is cut off in early spring and the rim of the caudex notched—new growing points will eventually result. The following spring the caudex is cut lengthwise, each piece with a growing point and these are then inserted as cuttings. Once rooted, all cuttings can then be potted on in the usual manner (see p. 29).

So far, attempts to grow lewisias under laboratory conditions (micropropagation techniques) have failed, but obviously if such a technique could be mastered it would be a most useful way of producing both virus-free stocks and increasing the rarer species, hybrids and cultivars.

PESTS AND DISEASES

The worst pests are various species of aphids and a regular programme of spraying has to be undertaken in order to control them—the only really safe sprays to use are those based on pyrethrum, since lewisias can be damaged by systemic insecticides. Spraying must continue all the year round. The deciduous species are the worse affected, especially during the winter period, when the aphids collect in the tight resting crowns.

Lewisia cotyledon and its hybrids and *L. tweedyi* may be attacked by

Plate 1

Lewisia rediviva subsp. *rediviva* (top)
Lewisia rediviva 'Jolon' (bottom)

CHRISTABEL KING

Plate 2

Lewisia brachycalyx   CHRISTABEL KING

the dianthus fly. This lays its eggs in the leaf-tip and the larvae burrow down the midrib and on into the caudex causing the eventual collapse of the plant. Systemic insecticides will control it, but, as mentioned above, lewisias can react adversely to these chemicals.

Lewisias sometimes suffer from an odd malaise which results in the leaves becoming mottled and then turning yellow and bright orange—photographs of plants in the wild often show the same symptoms. The cause is unknown but all plants showing such symptoms should be burnt, along with the compost—the condition is highly contagious.

CULTIVATION REQUIREMENTS OF INDIVIDUAL SPECIES (alphabetical)

Lewisia brachycalyx. This species is difficult to maintain in cultivation. Plants often take up to five years to build up a reasonably sized crown, then they flower profusely, set seed and promptly die.

Plants recently introduced by Sally Walker from Tucson, Arizona are the true species, but plants formerly in cultivation, under the name *L. brachycalyx*, are almost certainly of hybrid origin. These and the Walker plants (as the seed parent) produce a range of hybrids. The long-cultivated '*L. brachycalyx*' will also hybridize readily with *L. cotyledon*, *L. longipetala*, *L. oppositifolia* and *L. rediviva*. The hybrids do not live long but are a joy whilst they are alive. During their summer dormancy these plants need just enough moisture in the plunge bed to keep them alive—if this is overdone they will decline more rapidly than any other lewisia.

Lewisia cantelovii. Treat as for *L. cotyledon*.

Lewisia columbiana (forms and hybrids). This species hates being under glass for the flower-stems become etiolated and out of proportion to the rest of the plant. However, grown in a trough or on a peat wall it is quite delightful. It is not necessary to grow it under an overhang, but a position shaded from the midday sun is preferable; under such conditions the flower-stems will remain short and in character with its wild counterpart. Pot-grown specimens in frames should be left uncovered as much as possible for the same reason— quite safe as the species is completely hardy. When grown in pots the compost should be the same as that recommended for *L. tweedyi*.

Lewisia congdonii. One of the winter-deciduous species; the plants go dormant in the early autumn, but despite this the compost and watering regime is as for *L. cotyledon*.

Lewisia cotyledon. This species, which exists in many forms in cultivation, is the most widely grown, indeed the easiest to grow. The general cultivation of *L. cotyledon* has already been described. The species is evergreen and like *L. columbiana* it is the easiest for outdoor cultivation, provided the centre of the leaf-rosettes can be kept dry during the winter—in wet districts a sheet of glass placed over the plants or some other form of protection is advisable. *Lewisia cotyledon* is also the best species for hybridization. Besides the great range of colours obtainable from crossing various forms, it will also cross readily with most other *Lewisia* species, with the exception of *L. tweedyi*; most of these hybrids only succeed by transferring *L. cotyledon* pollen on to the other species (i.e. as the male parent) and not vice versa. Compost is the same as for *L. tweedyi*.

Lewisia disepala. This is a very rare species in cultivation, like *L. kelloggii* and *L. maguirei*. If these plants can be obtained then it is probably best to treat them as for *L. rediviva*. It is a good practice, if you are not sure of the dormancy water requirement of such species, carefully to remove some of the soil and very gently press the caudex. If it feels at all soft then water the plunge material, if firm then leave well alone. (Note—if the caudex of *L. rediviva* feels soft, *do not* water the plant!)

Lewisia kelloggii. See *L. disepala*.

Lewisia leeana. Although in some places in the wild this species grows together with *L. cotyledon*, strangely its watering requirements are different. The plants have a very small root-system and seem to resent excess moisture at any time; however, apart from this, the general treatment is as for *L. cotyledon*.

Hybrids between *L. cotyledon* and *L. leeana* occur naturally in the wild. In cultivation hybrids can only be obtained by using *L. cotyledon* as the male parent. One of the finest of such hybrids is 'Margaret Williams' which is a very long-lived plant, making few offsets and having a huge, rather ugly, caudex 7–8 cm across and with a relatively small root-system. It should be treated as for *L. leeana*, giving it very little water at any time.

Lewisia longipetala. This is an odd species which Mrs Margaret Williams of Sparks, Nevada, who knows the plant in the wild, describes as erratic. Plants go dormant in the late autumn, dying back to a small tuft of leaves which persists over the winter. In the late spring it is normally the last species to start growing, or it can sometimes remain as a tuft for a year until the following spring. If it does grow it requires moisture all summer, when it will flower almost continuously, virtually until a few days before it suddenly goes dormant once more.

All the time it is in flower it gives plenty of pollen for hybridization purposes as well as being a good female (seed) parent for most other species—but not *L. tweedyi*. In fact *L. longipetala* makes an excellent parent and has given rise to some fine long-flowering hybrids such as 'Pinkie' (now sadly virused), 'Ben Chace', 'Ashwood Pearl', 'Matthew', and many more either not distinct enough or good enough to name. All thrive in the standard lewisia compost.

Lewisia maguirei. See under *L. disepala*.

Lewisia nevadensis. There is no finer sight than this species in full flower. *Lewisia nevadensis* is easily grown and the form generally seen is a robust plant, frequently despised because it is easy and sets masses of seeds. However, some forms are extremely difficult to maintain—for example, a small pink-flushed white one which has been introduced from Mt. McCloud. All forms require a good summer rest in a damp plunge bed. All attempts to colonize *L. nevadensis* in a bulb frame seem to have failed, the plants generally dying during the winter.

Lewisia nevadensis 'Rosea' is a mystery which seems to be a form of *L. nevadensis*. It is a very desirable pot-plant, but unfortunately the seed has a poor germination rate.

Lewisia oppositifolia. The typical form of this species rarely does well in cultivation. However, 'Richeyi' is a smaller, neater plant which is easy to grow in the standard compost. The plunge material should be kept just damp during the summer dormancy period.

Lewisia pygmaea. It would seem logical that one of the most widespread species in the wild, *L. pygmaea*, would need diverse treatments in cultivation, but this is not so. These tiny plants need to be kept just moist throughout the year, using the standard lewisia potting compost, but they should never be overpotted. They often produce an occasional flower throughout the summer. One unusual form has come into cultivation from Arizona; it is coarse in comparison with most forms and comes into flower much later, starting at about the same time as *L. longipetala*. Oddly enough *L. longipetala* is thought to be close to, and indeed was once included in, *L. pygmaea*, and yet it is not known to cross with any forms of the latter, including the odd Arizona form.

Lewisia rediviva. This is the easiest lewisia to grow provided certain rules are obeyed. The compost should be a variant on the standard one with 1 part John Innes potting compost No. 3, to 2 parts mixed sand and grit. From the time the flowers fade until the autumn no water should be given, either to the pot or to the plunge material. In early autumn the plants should be completely repotted into hand-damp compost, given one good watering after two weeks and kept in damp plunge over winter. When renewed growth is obvious, usually at the end of February, they should be well watered. This is one of the most delightful and rewarding members of the genus.

Lewisia serrata. Treat as for *L. cotyledon* and *L. cantelovii*.

Lewisia sierrae. This is one of the smaller species. Two forms are in general cultivation. One has minute tight leaf-rosettes and many tiny white flowers—it was originally found in thick black mud in the wild and is easy to grow, being given only one or two waterings during the summer. The other form is much looser with pink flowers and is much more difficult to grow and must have a dry rest period. Neither form seems to hybridize with other species (but see p. 131) although both set a lot of seed. Young plants are very slow-growing and should not be pricked out for three or four years.

Lewisia stebbinsii. A small, slow-growing species that will grow under the same general conditions as *L. oppositifolia*. Seed set is very erratic, especially as the plants become older.

Lewisia triphylla. This interesting species forms a tiny rounded rootstock looking like a young bulb. Unfortunately, plants never seem to do well in cultivation; although they do not die out they never seem to get going. In the wild this species inhabits damp places.

Lewisia tweedyi. This very beautiful species deserves to be in any collection of lewisias. Although reasonably easy to grow it does demand special care and attention to succeed well. The standard compost needs to be adjusted to 1 part John Innes potting compost No. 3, to 2 parts peat and 2 parts grit. This is also the best compost mixture for *L. columbiana*, but there any similarity in their treatment ends, for they are quite different in their other requirements. *Lewisia tweedyi* makes large plants with extensive root-systems. The pots should be plunged in full light but shaded from strong spring sunshine. Strictly no water should be applied directly to the pots after seed has been set, until mid-autumn, and also no water during the winter months. Otherwise the potting regime is the same as for *L. cotyledon*.

HYBRIDIZING

It has already been noted how promiscuous lewisias are in cultivation and that a number of excellent hybrids have arisen spontaneously. The majority of such hybrids are sterile and can only be increased vegetatively.

Most plants lose vigour in time through constant vegetative reproduction; lewisias appear to lose vigour very rapidly indeed! It is therefore desirable that each generation of lewisia enthusiasts should, from time to time, try to repeat former successful crosses. This should be undertaken with some purpose in mind; for instance, crossing a species that is shy to produce offsets in order to get offspring which can be more readily propagated. All but the very best seedlings should be ruthlessly destroyed—this is imperative with the vast numbers of *L. cotyledon* hybrids that are raised each year. Colour is of course important, but so is flower shape and texture. A perfect flower should be full, nicely rounded with overlapping petals and the flowers should hold their heads up well on firm stalks. They should also be firm in texture and weather-proof, for even when grown under glass some of them will not stand the extra atmospheric moisture which results from the necessary 'damping down' of an alpine house in summer.

Once you have started on the quest for perfecting a strain (crossing the best with the best from each batch) watch carefully for genetic defects that may manifest themselves, perhaps through inbreeding. Offending plants should be destroyed, the crossing programme stopped and some fresh stock brought in for hybridization purposes—eventually your desired plants will begin to appear again.

It is always important to maintain stocks of the wild species and not lose one's collection in a maze of hybrids—wild-collected seed introduces 'fresh blood' into collections.

TAXONOMIC TREATMENT

Lewisia F. Pursh, Fl. Amer. Sept. 368 (1814); J. Torrey & A. Gray, Fl. N. Amer. 1: 677–8 (1840); T. Howell in Erythea 1: 29–41 (1893); K. Brandegee in Proc. Calif. Acad. Sci. ser. 2, 4: 86–91 (1894); B.L. Robinson in A. Gray, Syn. Fl. N. Amer. 1: 266–9 (1897); W.L. Jepson, Fl. Calif. 1: 463–80 (1914); R.S. Ferris in L. Abrams, Ill. Fl. Pacific States 2: 131 (1944); C.L. Hitchcock et al., Vasc. Pl. Pacific Northwest 2: 225–49 (1964); R.C. Elliott in Bull. Alpine Gard. Soc. 34: 1–76 (1966), and as a separate booklet (1966), 2nd edn (1978); J.E. Hohn, Biosystematic studies of the genus Lewisia, section Cotyledon (Portulacaceae) — Ph.D. thesis, Univ. of Washington (1975); J. Cobb Colley & B. Mineo in Pacific Hort. 46(2): 40–9 (1985). Type species: *L. rediviva* Pursh.
Oreobroma T. Howell in Erythea 1: 31 (1893).
Erocallis P.A. Rydberg in Bull. Torrey Bot. Club 33: 139 (1906).

GENERIC DESCRIPTION. *Glabrous, succulent, perennial herbs*; root-stock fleshy, usually branched, crowned by a short caudex. *Basal leaves* (if present) clustered at the apex of the caudex, evergreen or dying away after flowering, usually numerous, arranged in a well-defined rosette or in a more irregular tuft, linear to spatulate or obovate, often expanded and hyaline at the base, margins entire or toothed. *Stem-leaves* usually reduced but sometimes well developed and similar to the basal leaves, mostly alternate but sometimes opposite or whorled. *Inflorescences* frequently paniculate or cymose, sometimes ± racemose or reduced to a single flower. *Bracts* subtending the flowers and the branches of the inflorescence alternate, opposite or whorled, entire or glandular-toothed. *Flowers* hermaphrodite, pedicellate or sessile (when the bracts immediately subtend the flower and appear to represent extra sepals). *Sepals* 2, persistent, small and greenish or purplish, or 2–9, rather large, petaloid and white or pale pink; margins entire, dentate or glandular-dentate. *Petals* (4–)5–19, thin in texture, often unequal, especially in width, white, pink, magenta or yellowish, often veined darker or sometimes striped. *Stamens* 5–50 with filiform filaments and versatile anthers. *Ovary* subglobose to ovoid; ovules few to many. *Style-branches* 3–8, fused at the base. *Capsule* circumscissile near the base and subsequently splitting lengthways. *Seeds* few to many, ovoid to reniform or suborbicular, usually black and glossy, minutely tuberculate, with or without a fleshy appendage (strophiole).

DISTRIBUTION. North America: Rocky Mountains, Cascade Range and Sierra Nevada. MAP 1.

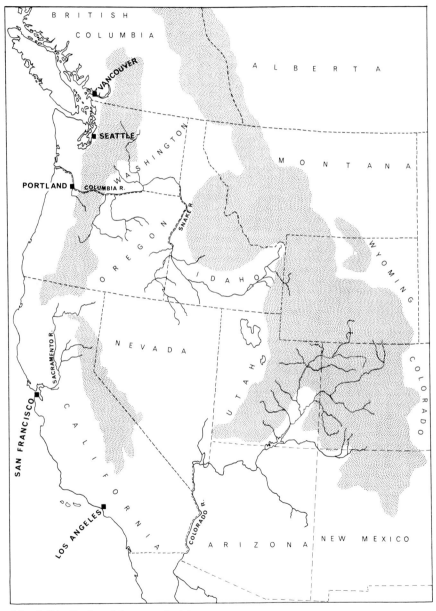

Map 1. Distribution of the genus *Lewisia*.

INFRAGENERIC CLASSIFICATION

There is no existing formal classification of *Lewisia* into subgenera, sections, etc., and it is perhaps unwise to suggest such a system at the present time, since thorough studies of various aspects of the genus such as cytology, palynology and biochemistry are required. R.C. Elliott (1966) has suggested that the genus could be divided into three groups 'according to their growth habits in nature'. These were I. the Cotyledon Group (*L. cantelovii, L. columbiana, L. congdonii, L. cotyledon, L. leeana* and *L. tweedyi*), II. the Pygmaea Group (*L. brachycalyx, L. kelloggii, L. nevadensis, L. oppositifolia, L. pygmaea, L. sierrae* and *L. triphylla*) and III. the Rediviva Group (*L. disepala, L. maguirei* and *L. rediviva*). J.E. Hohn (1975), in a study of the evergreen lewisias recognized a section *Cotyledon* with the same species content as Elliott, except for *L. tweedyi* which she placed in a separate section, *Strophiolum*.

On the basis of the known, mainly morphological, characters it is clear that some natural groups can be recognized.

Lewisia tweedyi is in several respects a very distinct species with no obvious relatives and should be segregated from the rest; furthermore, it does not hybridize with any other *Lewisia*. The mainly evergreen species form a fairly convincing group of six, with *L. cotyledon* as the most well-known representative; *L. congdonii*, although deciduous, clearly fits in with this group. The rest of the species are all deciduous types. Of these, *L. rediviva* and its two allies (as in Elliott's Group III) may be put together because of the papery sepals and jointed pedicels which break off and allow the whole flower to fall as a wind-blown seed dispersal unit. *Lewisia pygmaea* is apparently one of a group of five closely related species, while *L. brachycalyx* and *L. kelloggii* also seem to be allied in certain ways, notably because of the fact that the flowers lack pedicels, so that the bracts and sepals are held close together and appear to form the outer whorl of the flower. The remaining species, *L. triphylla* and *L. oppositifolia*, have no obvious affinities with any other species and not a great deal with each other, although they could be placed together since they both have stems bearing well-developed opposite or whorled leaves; probably the best approach is to regard them as belonging to monotypic groups, at least until they can be studied in greater depth.

It is suggested that, on the basis of present knowledge, the infrageneric classification of *Lewisia* should consist of two subgenera, one containing only *L. tweedyi* and the other subdivided into six sections as follows:

Lewisia F. Pursh

subgenus *Lewisia*.   Seeds without a fleshy appendage, non-tuberculate.

section *Lewisia*.   Plants deciduous; pedicels jointed, the whole flower falling in the fruiting stage; sepals 2–9, scarious.
    1. *L. rediviva**
    2. *L. maguirei*
    3. *L. disepala*

section *Brachycalyx* B. Mathew.   Plants deciduous; inflorescence 1-flowered; flowers sessile, the bracts and sepals touching.
    4. *L. kelloggii*
    5. *L. brachycalyx**

section *Erocallis* B. Mathew.   Plants deciduous, with a globose tuber; stem-leaves well developed, usually in a whorl of three.
    6. *L. triphylla**

section *Oppositifolia* B. Mathew.   Plants deciduous; stem-leaves well developed, borne in pairs; pedicels long and slender.
    7. *L. oppositifolia**

40

section *Pygmaea* B. Mathew.	Plants deciduous; flowers solitary or inflorescences few-branched; leaves usually rather narrow.	8. *L. nevadensis* 9. *L. longipetala* 10. *L. sierrae* 11. *L. pygmaea** 12. *L. stebbinsii*
section *Cotyledon* J.E. Hohn ex B. Mathew.	Plants evergreen; inflorescences tall, much branched; leaves usually rather broad.	13. *L. congdonii* 14. *L. columbiana* 15. *L. leeana* 16. *L. cantelovii* 17. *L. serrata* 18. *L. cotyledon**
subgenus *Strophiolum* (J.E. Hohn) ex B. Mathew.	Seeds tuberculate with a prominent fleshy appendage.	19. *L. tweedyi**

Species marked with an asterisk are the type species of the subgenera or sections.

Key to the Subgenera and Sections

1. Seeds with a prominent fleshy appendage (strophiole)
   subgen. **Strophiolum**
   Seeds without a fleshy appendage .... (subgen. **Lewisia**)   2

2. Sepals 2–9, papery, white or pink; pedicels jointed, allowing the whole flower to fall in fruit .... sect. **Lewisia**
   Sepals 2, green or purplish-tinged; pedicels not jointed   3

41

3. Flowers without a pedicel, the 2 bracts and 2 sepals thus touching
   sect. **Brachycalyx**
   Flowers with a pedicel, the 2 bracts and 2 sepals thus separated .   4

4. Stem-leaves present and well developed, opposite or whorled   5
   Stem-leaves, if present, much reduced and usually alternate   6

5. Leaves usually in whorls of 3; plant with a ± globose tuber
   sect. **Erocallis**
   Leaves in pairs; plant with a fleshy branched root-stock
   sect. **Oppositifolia**

6. Plants evergreen (except *L. congdonii*), rather tall in flower with widely
   branched inflorescences and usually rather broad leaves (except *L.
   leeana*) .... sect. **Cotyledon**
   Plants deciduous, low-growing with few-branched inflorescences and
   very narrow leaves .... sect. **Pygmaea**

Key to the Species

Note: hybrids are unlikely to key out satisfactorily.

1. Plant with a ± globose tuber; basal leaves not present at flowering time;
   stem-leaves in a pair or whorl of 3 .... 6. **L. triphylla**
   Plants with elongated fleshy, usually branched root-stocks; basal
   leaves present at flowering time; stem-leaves, if present, not paired or
   whorled (except in 7. *L. oppositifolia*)   2

2. Leaves dying away at or soon after flowering time   3
   Leaves in evergreen rosettes, not dying away in summer   14

3. Bracts produced immediately below the sepals with no intervening
   pedicel   4
   Bracts carried some distance below the sepals, separated from them by
   a distinct pedicel   5

4. Flowers 2–3 cm in diameter; sepals toothed, sometimes glandular;
   leaves spatulate, obtuse or retuse .... 4. **L. kelloggii**
   Flowers 3–5(–6) cm in diameter; sepals neither toothed nor glandular;
   leaves oblanceolate, tapering at the apex .... 5. **L. brachycalyx**

5. Sepals 2–9, papery, white or pinkish; in fruit, pedicel breaking off with
   whole flower attached   6
   Sepals 2, not papery, green, or green suffused with purple; in fruit,
   pedicel not breaking off, but the old flowers remaining attached to
   the inflorescence   8

6. Sepals 2; flowers solitary; petals 5–7 .... 3. **L. disepala**
   Sepals 3–9; flowers 1–3; petals 7–19 7

7. Petals 7–9; bracts ovate to ovate-oblong; leaves narrowly oblanceolate,
   flattish .... 2. **L. maguirei**
   Petals 12–19; bracts subulate or linear-lanceolate; leaves ± terete
   1. **L. rediviva**

8. Stem-leaves well developed, produced in 1–3 pairs
   7. **L. oppositifolia**
   Stem-leaves, if present at all, alternate and usually much reduced   9

9. Inflorescences 20–60 cm long, erect or suberect with many flowers in
   loose panicles; leaves oblanceolate, 10–50 mm wide
   13. **L. congdonii**
   Inflorescences at most 15 cm long, decumbent or suberect with 1–11
   flowers; leaves linear, linear-lanceolate, spatulate, obovate or
   oblanceolate, usually less than 10 mm wide 10

10. Leaves oblanceolate, obovate or spatulate, 3–11.5(–20) mm wide;
    flowers *c.* 2 cm in diameter; petals rich carmine with a large white
    basal zone .... 12. **L. stebbinsii**
    Leaves linear or linear-oblanceolate, 1–6 mm wide; flowers 0.9–4 cm in
    diameter; petals white, pale pink or magenta but if richly coloured
    then flowers rather small (0.9–2 cm in diameter) and petals lacking a
    large white basal zone 11

11. Flowers 2–4 cm in diameter, or if only 2–2.5 cm, then petals usually
    pure white and sepals not toothed; pedicels 1–4 cm long   12
    Flowers 0.9–2 cm in diameter, but if 2 cm, then petals usually pale to
    deep pink or magenta and sepals toothed; pedicels 1.5–7(–10) mm
    long 13

12. Sepals green, entire or with a few obscure non-glandular teeth; petals
    usually pure white .... 8. **L. nevadensis**
    Sepals strongly stained with purple, conspicuously glandular-dentate;
    petals usually very pale pink .... 9. **L. longipetala**

13. Flowers usually 0.9–1.1 cm in diameter; sepals entire or slightly
    dentate .... 10. **L. sierrae**
    Flowers usually 1.5–2 cm in diameter; sepals usually dentate,
    sometimes glandular-dentate .... 11. **L. pygmaea**

14. Flowers 4–5.5(–7) cm in diameter; bracts entire .... 19. **L. tweedyi**
    Flowers 1–4 cm in diameter; bracts glandular-denticulate 15

15. Leaves linear and ± terete, only 2–3.5 mm wide .... 15. **L. leeana**
    Leaves ± flat or slightly channelled on upper surface, spatulate,
    oblanceolate, obovate or linear, 3–40 mm wide 16

16. Leaves 3–8 mm wide with smooth margins .... 14. **L. columbiana**
    Leaves 5–40 mm wide with dentate or undulate margins but if smooth-
    margined then 1 cm or more wide 17

17. Flowers 2–4 cm in diameter; petals pinkish purple, apricot, yellow or
    pinkish orange, often with a broad longitudinal stripe of colour
    18. L. cotyledon
    Flowers 1–1.5 cm in diameter; petals white or pale pink and finely
    veined darker but not with a broad stripe of colour 18

18. Leaves 5–17 mm wide, spatulate with a nearly orbicular blade,
    narrowed abruptly to the long-tapering petiole; margins
    conspicuously but rather finely dentate .... 16. **L. cantelovii**
    Leaves 10–15(–20) mm wide, narrowly obovate, narrowing gradually
    to the base; margins very coarsely triangular-dentate
    17. L. serrata

1. LEWISIA REDIVIVA

Lewisia rediviva, the type species of the genus and known as the bitterroot, is perhaps the most beautiful of all the lewisias with its huge soft satiny pink or white flowers which look extremely like cactus flowers in their petal texture and clarity of colour. Bitterroot is perhaps a rather dull name for such an attractive species but it gives an indication that there is some other interest in the plant in addition to its undeniably high aesthetic appeal. *Lewisia* roots were, and probably still are to some extent, eaten by the western North American Indians and are usually described as having a bitter taste, hence the name, although one author describes the flavour as agreeable when boiled. It appears that the bitterroot was mainly used as a food rather than for medicinal purposes and seems to have been of significant importance, for it has been noted that certain Indians considered it to be one of the Great Spirit's foremost gifts. The main food value appears to lie in the fact that there is a useful starch content; moreover the roots are fairly sizeable and contain no tough or woody tissues. There are several reported methods of preparing the roots for culinary purposes including boiling and drying for later use, boiling with meat, frying with fish or making into flour for use in soups or bread: occasionally the roots were eaten raw. They were sometimes also eaten mixed with berries or meat and it is said that in modern times the Flathead Indians of Montana have been known to eat them with cream and sugar. One of the Indian names which is recorded most frequently on specimens is *spat'lum* or *spitlem* (and various other spellings) which appears to mean bitterroot, so that this can be taken to be the original vernacular name of the plant. Other names which can be found in literature include reviving lewisia, resurrection flower and rock rose, but they are seldom encountered, and in British horticultural circles I have not heard of the species being referred to as anything other than *Lewisia rediviva*. The French name used by the early settlers was *racine amère*, literally, bitterroot.

There is little evidence that the bitterroot is of medicinal value, although it has been reported that the roots are sometimes chewed to alleviate sore throats (Daubenmire, 1975) and the Flathead Indians are reported to have drunk an infusion of the roots for heart trouble and pleurisy (Hart, 1976). In *Vascular Plants of the Pacific Northwest* (Hitchcock *et al.*, 1964) it is noted that the roots are 'dug usually early in spring as the leaves are developing and long before flowering time, when the root becomes most bitter. The Indians know (or believe) that only certain areas produce palatable roots. The roots are peeled and boiled, and either eaten immediately or dried and used later, when they are again cooked. The modern Indian preserves his excess roots in the deep freeze.'

R. Daubenmire (1975) in an excellent study of *L. rediviva* is not, however, of the same opinion concerning the bitter flavour and remarks that even after chewing for some time there is no more than a faint bitterness and that the blackish bark is tasteless. Most accounts suggest that the bitter taste can be removed by boiling whereas Daubenmire found that, if anything, a definite bitterness developed as a result of boiling the roots. Jeff Hart (1976), in his fascinating account of the Indian uses of plants in Montana, states that the Indian women dug up the plants before they bloomed because at that time the blackish bark could be easily removed. The roots were washed and peeled and sometimes the inner core was removed, since this was believed to be responsible for much of the bitter taste. The Kutenais and Flathead tribes apparently regarded *L. rediviva* as one of the most important root-crops and there was an annual two day celebration, the First Roots Ceremony, held in May to herald the new season. The chief, advised by an elderly woman as to the readiness of the 'crop', would announce the start of the ceremony and the opening of the new year's digging. Prayers were offered and there was a feast of bitterroot broth containing lewisia roots stewed with grouse and deer.

It is perhaps rather surprising that *L. rediviva* is still such a common plant in the wild, for the collecting activities of the Indians must have accounted for thousands, if not millions, of plants each year. Hart (1976) records that the women 'often worked three or four days to fill a fifty-pound sack. Each woman gathered at least two sacks, enough to sustain two people through the winter. A sack of bitterroots was worth a lot. Geyer, an early botanical explorer, said that 'one sack was worth a horse'. Hart also notes that special digging tools were used by the Indians, one was a 90 cm willow stick with a fire-hardened digging end and a deer antler handle, while the other was made from elk antler and was about 38 cm long. More recently, however, they have used iron ones crafted by blacksmiths.

Lewisia rediviva was first collected as a botanical specimen on 1 July 1806 by Captain Meriwether Lewis during the famous Lewis and

Plate 3

Lewisia oppositifolia (left)
Lewisia oppositifolia 'Richeyi' (right)

CHRISTABEL KING

Plate 4

Lewisia pygmaea (top)
Lewisia nevadensis (bottom)

CHRISTABEL KING

Plate 5

Lewisia longipetala   CHRISTABEL KING

Plate 6

Lewisia sierrae (top)
Lewisia stebbinsii (bottom)

CHRISTABEL KING

Clark expedition which crossed America from the east to the Pacific and back using the great Missouri and Columbia river systems. The specimen was collected on the return journey at or near the junction of the Bitterroot River and Lolo Creek, about 19 km south of Missoula in Montana. Lewis had, however, encountered the plant on the westward journey in the previous year when the expedition was camped in western Montana in the Big Hole Valley. There was a minor skirmish with some Indians who fled and left behind some bags containing roots, some of which were described as fusiform and about 15 cm long, and were, as Lewis later discovered, used as food after being boiled. He prepared some and noted that they had a bitter taste, but were much appreciated by the Indians.

In Montana, *L. rediviva* seems to be very widespread and common in the south and west and in fact it has one of the widest distributions in the genus, from southern British Columbia in the Kootenay and Okanagan Valleys, south into Washington, Idaho, Montana, Oregon, Wyoming, California, Nevada, Utah, north-west Colorado and northern Arizona. Daubenmire (1975) has studied the ecology and distribution in considerable detail and indicates that the species shows a clear preference for 'dry climates west of the continental divide where the limited rainfall comes mainly in the cold season'. However, it is noted that the Yellowstone Valley of southern Montana is an exception where the rainfall is heaviest in May and June. The comparatively wet western slopes of the Coast Ranges in California and Oregon are avoided by *L. rediviva*, as are the western slopes of the Cascades in Washington. The habitat is normally in fully exposed rocky or sandy places, although it may also be found on heavier soils, and there are records of its occurring in both acid and alkaline conditions, so the species shows a tolerance of a wide range of habitats. The main factor, it seems, and the one which dictates the cultivation method, is the summer drought when the plant dies down to its fleshy root-stock and has little or no moisture around the crown. In cultivation in damper climates the most common cause of failure is rotting at the crown brought about by excess moisture, rather than by cold, for there is no doubt that *L. rediviva* is extremely hardy.

The epithet *rediviva* was given to the bitterroot by Frederick Pursh for its remarkable ability to withstand the trauma of being turned into a herbarium specimen. In his *Flora Americae Septentrionalis* of 1814 he noted that 'this elegant plant would be a very desirable addition to the ornamental perennials, since, if once introduced, it would be easily kept and propagated, as the following circumstances will clearly prove. The specimen with roots taken out of the Herbarium of M. Lewis Esq. was planted by Mr McMahon of Philadelphia, and vegetated for more than one year.' According to Dr Elliott Coues (1899) the Lewis type specimen, which was collected on 1 July 1806, consists of several flowers only, presumably all the root-stocks having been removed and planted by Mr McMahon, an act which would today be considered sacrilegious in a herbarium!

W.J. Hooker underlined this tenacity for life on the part of *L. rediviva* in *Curtis's Botanical Magazine* for 1863 where he provided an account of the 'Reviving Lewisia' to accompany the beautiful illustration (t.5395) by W.H. Fitch. This was apparently the first published coloured illustration of a lewisia. Hooker wrote 'We have ourselves had dried specimens, preserved two or more years in the herbarium, still sending up fresh crops of leaves. The specimen from which our figure was taken at Kew is one of many which, when gathered with a view of being preserved for the herbarium, in British Columbia by Dr Lyall RN of the Boundary Expedition [1860], was immersed in boiling water on account of its well-known tenacity of life. More than a year and a half after, it notwithstanding showed symptoms of vitality, and produced its beautiful flowers in great profusion in May of the present year [1863], in the Royal Gardens of Kew.' It was this resuscitated specimen which was painted for the *Botanical Magazine* plate!

Lewisia rediviva cannot readily be confused with any other species, so there is little value in presenting a lengthy discussion about the distinguishing features, other than to say that it is almost certainly most closely related to *L. maguirei* and *L. disepala* but clearly differs from both in having more sepals and petals to its much larger flowers. All three species have flowers which, once they have withered, fall off with their pedicels still attached, to be blown by the wind for the purposes of seed dispersal. Daubenmire (1975) notes that in *L. rediviva*, the structure which is formed by the dried twisted corolla, the widely expanded papery sepals and the pedicel, is roughly spherical in outline and weighs only about 0.1 g so that it is ideally suited for dispersal by wind. The corolla, together with the upper cap-like part of the ovary, soon becomes detached from the rest resulting in the seeds becoming exposed and they can then be released gradually as the dispersal unit rolls along. Almost certainly *L. disepala* and *L. maguirei* behave in much the same way although they appear not to have been the subjects of any detailed studies.

Not surprisingly, the beauty of *L. rediviva*, and its attraction as a garden plant, was recognized early on and a First Class Certificate was bestowed upon it by the Royal Horticultural Society in 1873. It is a variable species in flower colour and form and as a result there have been named selections. One of these, 'Winifred Herdman', was a wild collected plant said to have originated in the Okanagan Valley in the 'dry belt' region of southern British Columbia, and was thought to be superior in the colour (soft pink) and size of its flowers (about 7.5 cm in diameter); this received an Award of Merit in 1927. More recently, a large flowered variant named 'Jolon' (PLATE 1) from an introduction by Wayne Roderick from Jolon, California, gained an Award of Merit in May 1976 when exhibited by Kath Dryden; the flowers of this were colour-matched as Red Group 55c in the RHS colour chart, but seedlings from it vary in colour from white to pink, although the very large flower size is retained. It appears that the natural variation of *L. rediviva* has some slight geographical significance and I have continued to recognize the diminutive variant subsp. *minor*, although Sean Hogan, who has studied the species over a wide area, tells me that it is probably not distinct. In *Vascular Plants of the Pacific Northwest* (Hitchcock *et al.*, 1964) it is noted that 'on the whole the flowers of the Rocky Mountain area tend to be more deeply pink than those from the E base of the Cascades', and Roy Davidson tells me that the plants in the Bitterroot Valley, Montana have particularly brightly coloured flowers. Montana has in fact bestowed upon the lovely *L. rediviva* a higher honour, for it is the State Flower.

Lewisia rediviva Pursh, Fl. Amer. Sept. 2: 368 (1814). Type: Montana, 'On the banks of Clarks river' (holotype PH).
L. alba Kellogg in Proc. Calif. Acad. Sci. 2: 115 (1861) (no specimen or location cited).
L. rediviva var. *flore albo* Hook. in Curtis's Bot. Mag. 89: t.5395 (1863).

DESCRIPTION. *Stemless deciduous perennial* up to 5 cm tall when in flower, the leaves forming compact tufts (not regular rosettes) early in the year and then dying away at or before flowering time, produced from a short simple or branched caudex and fleshy branching taproot. *Leaves* many, linear or clavate, subterete, 1.5–5 cm long, 2–3 mm wide, obtuse or subacute with no petiole but with a broad hyaline base, fleshy, entire, withering as the flowers reach anthesis. *Inflorescences* consisting of 1-flowered scapes, the peduncles 1–3 cm long. *Stem-leaves* absent. *Bracts* 4–7(–8) in a whorl, subulate or linear-lanceolate, 4–10 mm long, scarious. *Pedicels* (1–)3–15(–30) mm long, jointed just above the bracts and readily breaking off after anthesis. *Flowers* 5–6(–7.5) cm in diameter. *Sepals* (4–)6–9, unequal, imbricate, white or pinkish, with a green or purplish mid-vein, broadly elliptic or ovate, rounded, 10–25 mm long, entire to erose. *Petals* 12–19, in various shades of rose-pink, purplish pink or white, elliptic, oblong or narrowly oblanceolate, 15–35 mm long, obtuse, truncate or rounded, entire or erose at the apex. *Stamens* 20–50 with the filaments united at the base. *Style* deeply divided into 4–9 white or pale pink branches. *Capsule* ovoid, 5–6 mm long. *Seeds* 6–25, black or dark brown, orbicular-reniform, 2–2.5 mm long, minutely papillate, shining.

A diminutive variant of *L. rediviva*, which occurs in a somewhat restricted area in Utah, Nevada and southern California, may be recognized as subsp. *minor*.

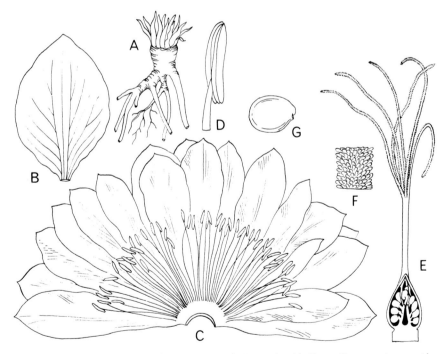

Lewisia rediviva subsp. **rediviva**. **A**, habit, ×⅓; **B**, sepal, ×1½; **C**, corolla, opened out, ×1½; **D**, anther, ×6; **E**, gynoecium with part of ovary removed, ×3; **F**, part of style-branch, ×20; **G**, seed, ×6.

a. subsp. **rediviva**

DESCRIPTION. *Leaves* linear, subterete. *Pedicels* more than 1 cm long. *Sepals* more than 15 mm long. *Petals* 18–35 mm long. *Stamens* 30–50.

ILLUSTRATIONS. PLATES 1, 13. Curtis's Bot. Mag. 89 t.5395 (1863); Bull. Alpine Gard. Soc. 4: 342 (1936); R.C. Elliot, Lewisias (ed. 2) 50 (1978); Pacific Hort. 46(2): 40, 41 (1985); Rocky Mountain Alpines (Amer. Rock Gard. Soc.) pl. 6 (1986).

FLOWERING PERIOD. (March–)May–July.

HABITAT. Open gravelly and rocky places; altitude 750–1850 m.

DISTRIBUTION CANADA: British Columbia. USA: from Washington, Idaho and Montana southwards to California, Arizona and Colorado and east to Wyoming.

b. subsp. **minor** (Rydberg) Holmgren in Leafl. W. Bot. 7(6): 136 (1954). Type: California, Ventura Co., July 1902, *A.D.E. Elmer* 3886 (holotype NY; isotype K).

L. minor Rydberg in N. Amer. Fl. 21: 327 (1932).

L. rediviva var. *minor* (Rydberg) Munz, Man. S. Calif. Bot. 158, 598 (1935).

DESCRIPTION. *Leaves* clavate to narrowly oblanceolate, grooved on the upper surface, rounded at the apex. *Pedicels* (1–)3–8 mm long. *Sepals* mostly 10–12 mm long, rarely to 15 mm. *Petals c.* 15 mm long. *Stamens* 20–30.

ILLUSTRATION. R.C. Elliott, Lewisias (ed. 2) 59 (1978).

FLOWERING PERIOD. May–June(–July).

HABITAT. Dry rocky places; altitude 1980–2745 m.

DISTRIBUTION. USA: S California, S and W Nevada, Utah (Tooele Co.).

2. LEWISIA MAGUIREI

This relative of *L. rediviva* is apparently a rare plant in its native haunts in Nevada and is quite probably not in cultivation at all at the present time. *Lewisia maguirei* was first collected by Dr Bassett Maguire and Professor Arthur H. Holmgren in 1945 in the Quinn Canyon Range of south-central Nevada and described as a new species by the latter in 1954. Professor Holmgren, who succeeded Dr Maguire as Curator of the Intermountain Herbarium, Utah State University, Logan, named it after his colleague who had transferred to the New York Botanical Garden where he became Curator. At the time of its collection it was said to be of frequent occurrence in loose denuded soil derived from limestone, associated with pine, juniper and sagebrush (*Artemisia* spp.) on a south facing ridge above Cherry

Creek Summit at an altitude of 2286 m. The same site has since been visited by the indefatigable traveller Mrs Margaret Williams who has supplied much useful information about lewisias in their wild state. She has reported that it occurs in bare situations in clay soil amid limestone rocks, wet in spring until the end of June but then drying out considerably in the later summer months.

Like *L. rediviva* this species is deciduous, the leaves dying away at or soon after flowering time, but they are quite different in shape from those of *L. rediviva* in which they are more or less cylindrical. *Lewisia maguirei* has flattish, linear-oblanceolate leaves with a conspicuous midrib. Its flowers are similar to those of *L. rediviva* in that they have petaloid, silvery-scarious, pinkish-tinged sepals; however, there are only three or four such sepals per flower in *L. maguirei* and usually six to nine in *L. rediviva*, although there may rarely be as few as four. The petals too differ in number and size, a maximum of nine having been recorded for *L. maguirei*, 8–12 mm in length, but 12–19 in *L. rediviva* and 15–35 mm in length, giving a much larger flower. Another important feature of *L. maguirei* is that its flowers are usually borne in cymes of two or three, rarely solitary, whereas those of *L. rediviva* are normally solitary. The four to eight whorled subulate or narrowly linear-lanceolate bracts of *L. rediviva* further serve to distinguish the two species, for *L. maguirei* has fewer, broader, oblong to oblong-ovate bracts, quite different in appearance. *L. disepala*, another related species, also has broader bracts than *L. rediviva* but this has only two sepals and is clearly distinct in other ways from both. Nevertheless, these three species do appear to form a close alliance within the genus.

There is no obvious reason why *L. maguirei* should be any more difficult to cultivate than its much better known relation *L. rediviva* which means that, when introduced, it is likely to be a plant for the alpine house, at least in those countries which cannot guarantee a warm dry summer. From the aesthetic point of view it should be equally attractive, although rather smaller in flower size than *L. rediviva*.

Lewisia maguirei A.H. Holmgren in Leafl. W. Bot. 7: 136 (1954). Type: Nevada, Nye Co., Quinn Canyon Range, 'above Cherry Creek Summit', 8 June 1945, *B. Maguire & A.H. Holmgren* 25346 (holotype NY; isotypes CAS, MO, UC, US, UTC).

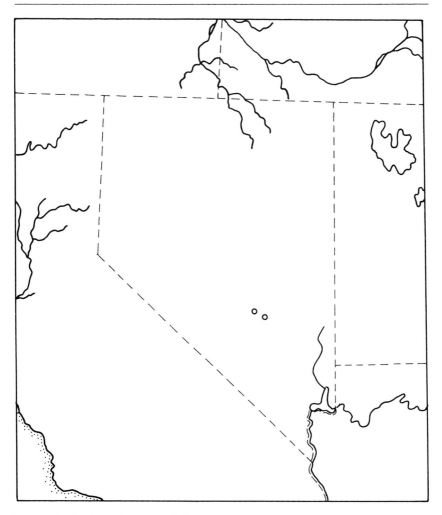

Map 2. Distribution of *Lewisia maguirei*.

DESCRIPTION. *Low, near-stemless, deciduous perennial* less than 5 cm in height when in flower with a loose tuft of basal leaves produced from a short caudex, and long fleshy branched taproots. *Basal leaves* fleshy, narrowly oblanceolate, 1–2 cm long, 1.5–3.5 mm wide, obtuse with a prominent midrib, shorter than the inflorescences and dying away at flowering time, forming loose tufts rather than clearly defined symmetrical rosettes. *Inflorescences* consisting of several short scapes 1.5–2 cm long, carrying usually 2 but sometimes 1 or 3 flowers in a cyme. *Bracts* oblong to oblong-ovate, 3–5 mm long, 2.5–3.5 mm wide, the lowest in a whorl of 3, the upper

53

ones subtending the pedicels, completely scarious. *Pedicels* stout, 3–9 mm long, articulated above the lowest whorl of bracts so that the whole flower-clusters, including the upper bracts, become detached in the fruiting stage. *Flowers* 2–3 cm in diameter. *Sepals* 3 or 4, petaloid, silvery-scarious with a pinkish suffusion, imbricate, broadly ovate, 8–12 mm long, 8–14 mm wide, rounded or emarginate, narrowed at the base into a short claw. *Petals* 7–9, white to pinkish, oblanceolate, 8–12 mm long, 4–6 mm wide, obtuse. *Stamens* 7–9. *Style* divided deeply into 4–6 branches. *Capsule* conical-oblong, 7–10 mm long. *Seeds* up to 10, 1.5–2.5 mm wide, smooth.

ILLUSTRATION. R.C. Elliott, Lewisias (ed. 2) 37 (1978).

FLOWERING PERIOD. June–July.

HABITAT. Open, gravelly-clay south facing slopes between *Pinus* and *Juniperus* on limestone derived soils; altitude 2286 m.

DISTRIBUTION. USA: Nevada (Nye Co., Quinn Canyon Range), known only from the type locality at Cherry Creek Summit. MAP 2, p. 53.

3. LEWISIA DISEPALA

This diminutive species was first described by Mary Katharine Brandegee in 1894 as a variety of *L. rediviva*, the varietal name *yosemitana* being chosen to indicate its origin in the Yosemite area of California where it was collected by Mrs Willie F. Dodd in 1891. Rydberg, in raising this to specific status in 1932, renamed it *L. disepala* for, under the International Rules of Nomenclature, he could not make use of the epithet *yosemitana* since it had already been used at specific level by Jepson in 1923. We now know that Jepson's *L. yosemitana* was a superfluous name, since that species had been described earlier as *L. kelloggii* by Brandegee in 1894. Thus, *L. yosemitana* Jepson is a synonym of *L. kelloggii*, and *L. rediviva* var. *yosemitana* Brandegee is a synonym of *L. disepala*.

As the name indicates, *L. disepala* has two sepals per flower, which is the normal complement in the genus, so it is therefore not a very helpful epithet. Per Axel Rydberg, in the *North American Flora* Vol. 21 (1932), recognized the genus *Oreobroma* Howell, with only two sepals per flower, as distinct from *Lewisia* which he keyed out on the basis of having six to eight sepals, but placed his new species *disepala* in *Lewisia*, together with *L. rediviva*, which may seem a curious logic, although he almost certainly had hit upon the correct relationship for *L. disepala*. In most of the *Lewisia* species which have two sepals, they are fairly inconspicuous whereas in *L. disepala* they are broad

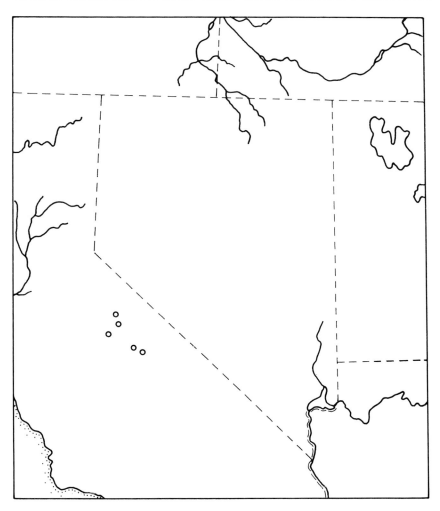

Map 3. Distribution of *Lewisia disepala*.

and quite obvious, spreading out in the fruiting stage and apparently forming part of the dispersal mechanism. As in *L. rediviva* and *L. maguirei* the pedicel breaks off releasing the whole flower; in the case of *L. disepala* it is reported (J.T. Howell in Elliott, *Lewisias* 31, 1978) that the 'sepals serve as wings by which the fruit is blown about and the seeds distributed'. Wayne Roderick (pers. comm.) tells me that usually by the beginning of June the plants have dried off and are not visible above ground for the rest of the year. The growing cycle of *L.*

55

disepala must therefore be restricted to some eight to ten weeks in spring, although there may be some root activity in autumn before the onset of winter.

Although Brandegee noted that the plant had only two sepals she obviously did not regard this as significant enough to distinguish it specifically from *L. rediviva*, which usually has six to nine sepals, and only rarely as few as four. In fact, within the small group of three species with articulated pedicels to which *L. disepala* belongs, it is distinct by virtue of its two sepals since the other related species, *L. maguirei*, has three or four. Apart from the sepal characters it can be distinguished from *L. rediviva* by its much smaller flowers, 2.5–3 (–3.5) cm in diameter, with only five to seven petals; the latter has 12 to 19 petals and a flower diameter of 5–6(–7.5) cm. *Lewisia disepala* appears to be more closely related to *L. maguirei* from Nevada, but the two sepals and solitary flowers serve to distinguish it from this species which normally has its flowers in cymes of two or three.

Lewisia disepala is a very restricted species in the wild, occurring in gravelly and rocky places on mountain summits around the Yosemite Valley in the Sierra Nevada at altitudes of about 1980–2600 m and usually flowering in April. Field notes supplied with a specimen from Mt. Watkins (*Sharsmith* 2034) suggest that it is locally abundant and that in some years at the higher altitudes may flower as late as June.

Undoubtedly it is an attractive dwarf species with short-stemmed pink flowers which are relatively large for the size of the plant. The narrow cylindrical leaves reach only 2 cm at most and shrivel away at flowering time like those of *L. rediviva*. Wayne Roderick describes it as being 'a gem of a plant when in bloom, which would stop an Alpine Garden Society show'! It is extremely rare in cultivation and it seems unlikely that it will ever become more than a specialist's subject for the alpine house.

Lewisia disepala Rydberg in N. Amer. Fl. 21: 328 (1932). Type: 'Yosemite Valley, California' (probably based on the type of *L. rediviva* var. *yosemitana*).

L. *rediviva* var. *yosemitana* K. Brandegee in Proc. Calif. Acad. Sci. Ser. 2, 4: 89, t.4 (1894). Type: California, 'collected somewhere about Yosemite Valley', 1891, *Mrs Willie F. Dodd* (Specimen destroyed in earthquake and fire in San Francisco in 1906).

DESCRIPTION. *Low, near-stemless, deciduous perennial* under 5 cm in height with a tuft of basal leaves produced from a short thick caudex which has fleshy branching roots. *Basal leaves* fleshy, terete, linear or slightly clavate, 8–20 mm long, obtuse, shorter than the inflorescences and dying away at flowering time, forming loose tufts, not clearly defined rosettes. *Inflorescences* consisting of several 1-flowered scapes 5–30 mm long. *Bracts* 2 or 3, ovate or lanceolate, 2–3 mm long, scarious. *Pedicels* 1–2 mm long, articulated so that in fruit the whole flower is shed. *Flowers* 2.5–3(–3.5) cm in diameter. *Sepals* 2, white or pinkish, broadly obovate or broadly ovate, 7–8 mm long, entire, rounded or sometimes emarginate, suberect at anthesis, spreading in fruit. *Petals* 5–7, pale rose-pink, oblanceolate or obovate, sometimes broadly so, 13–18 mm long, obtuse. *Stamens* 10–15. *Style* shortly divided, purplish. *Capsule* broadly ellipsoid. *Seeds* 11–15, black, rounded-reniform, 1.2–1.5 mm long.

ILLUSTRATION. P.A. Munz, Calif. Mountain Wildflowers 30, pl. 11 (1963); R.C. Elliott, Lewisias (ed. 2) 31 (1978) [line drawing].

FLOWERING PERIOD. February–April(–June).

HABITAT. Rocky, gravelly or sandy places near snowline, on granite formations; altitude 1980–2590 m.

DISTRIBUTION. USA: California (Sierra Nevada), known only from exposed mountain summits around Yosemite valley. MAP 3, p. 55.

4. LEWISIA KELLOGGII

Although it was named and given formal botanical recognition over 90 years ago from specimens gathered in the Sierra Nevada in 1870, this distinctive species has never become well established in cultivation. Even at the present time, when the genus is probably at a peak of popularity, it is extremely rare in the collections of a few alpine specialists, which is where it seems likely to remain for it is clearly not an easy plant to accommodate in cultivation. It was named by K. Brandegee after its collector Dr Albert Kellogg, a medical doctor and botanist who was born in Connecticut in 1813 but spent much of his later life, until his death in 1887, botanizing in California, illustrating and describing the flora in rich and enjoyable prose such as is to be found in his *Forest Trees of California* (1882).

Lewisia kelloggii is an attractive plant, making rosettes of spreading spatulate leaves adpressed to the ground, amid which rest the very short-stemmed white flowers which are 2–3 cm in diameter. Wayne Roderick notes (pers. comm.) that as the leaves grow they push away

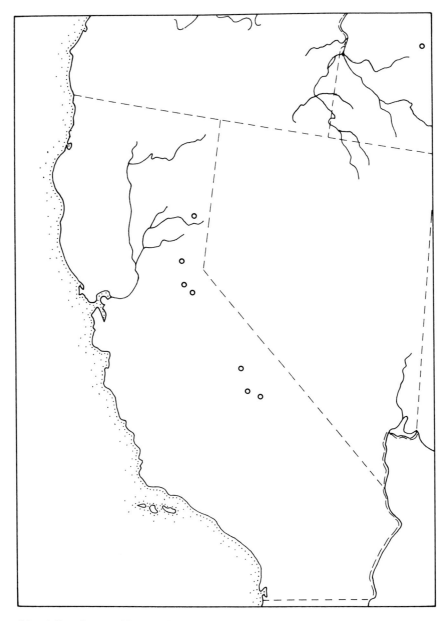

Map 4. Distribution of *Lewisia kelloggii*.

all the small rocks so that after dying down again there are small circles of sand where the rosettes have been. It is a very distinct species which has been compared with *L. rediviva* but it differs markedly from this in having flowers with no pedicels, the two bracts being situated immediately beneath the two sepals. In *L. rediviva* there are several subulate bracts in a whorl, separated from the flower by a pedicel at least 1 cm long, and there are six to nine sepals. In fact the bracts of *L. kelloggii* are so sepal-like that in the original description Brandegee did not distinguish between them and counted the sepals as four in number. The leaves of the two species are also very different, those of *L. kelloggii* being flat and spatulate while those of *L. rediviva* are subterete. In short, there are few features which the two species have in common, apart from being deciduous and low-growing. More closely related, in terms of numbers of coincidental features, is *L. brachycalyx* which has a similar number and arrangement of bracts, sepals and petals and a rosette-forming habit with short peduncles bearing solitary flowers, although here again there are plenty of distinguishing features. *Lewisia brachycalyx* has, on the whole, much larger flowers, some 3–6 cm in diameter, and the sepals are entire, not toothed as in *L. kelloggii*. The leaves too, in typical plants, are quite different in shape, those of *L. kelloggii* being spatulate with a rounded or notched apex while in *L. brachycalyx* they are oblanceolate and taper more gradually to the apex.

Lewisia kelloggii has a disjunct distribution, being found in the northern half of the Sierra Nevada and in the mountains of central Idaho. It grows in gritty granitic sand with very sharp drainage, moist in spring but drying out in the summer months, a combination of conditions which apparently make its cultivation a skilled and exacting task.

Lewisia kelloggii K. Brandegee in Proc. Calif. Acad. Sci. Ser. 2, 4: 88 (1894). Type: California, Sierra Nevada, Placer Co., Cisco ('Camp Yuba'), 27 June 1870, *Dr Albert Kellogg* (?CAS).

L. rediviva var. *yosemitana* H.M. Hall, Yosemite Fl. 84 (1912), non K. Brandegee (1894) (which is *L. disepala*).

L. yosemitana Jepson, Man. Fl. Pl. Calif. 352 (1923). Type: California, Mariposa Co., Yosemite, El Capitan, *Jepson* 4357 (JEPS).

Oreobroma kelloggii (K. Brandegee) Rydberg in N. Amer. Fl. 21: 326 (1932).

59

O. yosemitana (K. Brandegee) Rydberg in N. Amer. Fl. 21: 326 (1932).

DESCRIPTION. *Near-stemless, deciduous perennial* up to 3 cm in height when in flower, with rosettes of basal leaves produced from a short, stout caudex with fleshy branching roots. *Basal leaves* many, spatulate, fleshy, 1–6.5 cm long, obtuse or retuse, the lower narrow portion petiole-like, forming definite rather neat rosettes, usually flat on the ground but sometimes suberect. *Inflorescences* consisting of 1-flowered scapes 0.5–5 cm long, usually shorter than the leaves. *Bracts* 2, opposite, ovate or oblong, acute, glandular-denticulate, situated immediately beneath the calyx, with no intervening pedicel. *Flowers* sessile, 2–3 cm in diameter. *Sepals* 2, pinkish, ovate-lanceolate or oblanceolate, 5–12 mm long, acute, irregularly toothed,

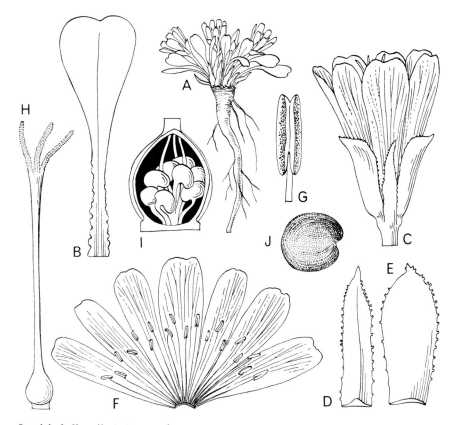

Lewisia kelloggii. A, habit, ×⅔; **B**, leaf, ×2; **C**, bud, ×2; **D**, bract, ×3; **E**, sepal, ×3; **F**, corolla, opened out, ×2; **G**, anther, ×8; **H**, gynoecium, ×4; **I**, ovary with part of the wall removed, ×12; **J**, seed, ×8.

sometimes with dark glandular teeth. *Petals* (5–)6–9(–12), white, obovate or oblanceolate, 10–15 mm long, 2–5 mm wide, obtuse, acute or truncate, variable in size in the same flower. *Stamens* 8–15(–26). *Style* divided into 3–5 branches. *Capsule* ovoid, *c.* 8 mm long. *Seeds* 12–15, black, suborbicular, *c.* 2 mm long, minutely tuberculate.

ILLUSTRATIONS. PLATES 14A, 14B. R.C. Elliott, Lewisias 27 (1966); H.W. Rickett, Wild Flowers of the U.S. 5(1): pl. 92 (1971).

FLOWERING PERIOD. Late May to early July.

HABITAT. Sandy or gravelly places, usually on granite formations and common on volcanic ash and other volcanic deposits, usually near melting snow; altitude 1370–2360 m.

DISTRIBUTION. USA: California (Sierra Nevada from Plumas Co., south to Mariposa Co.), C Idaho (in Valley Co., Elmore Co. and Custer Co.). MAP 4, p. 58.

5. LEWISIA BRACHYCALYX

The specific epithet of *L. brachycalyx*, meaning a short calyx, is not particularly instructive since the two sepals of this attractive lewisia are really no shorter than in several other species. One of the distinctive features does, however, partly concern the calyx, for at first sight it would appear that the calyx consists of four sepals. In fact, it is the two bracts which give this impression, for they are situated immediately beneath the two sepals with no intervening pedicel. This arrangement is unusual in *Lewisia* and is found only in this species and *L. kelloggii*, which is possibly the most closely related

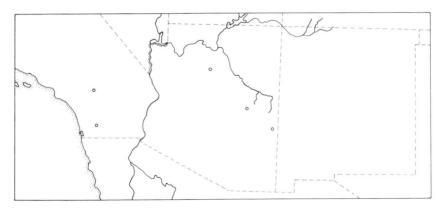

Map 5. Distribution of *Lewisia brachycalyx*.

to *L. brachycalyx*, although there is no great difficulty in distinguishing between them. The flower size alone is diagnostic, 3–6 cm across in *L. brachycalyx* and only 2–3 cm in *L. kelloggii*; but if there is any doubt, then the entire sepals of the flower will further distinguish it from *L. kelloggii* in which they are dentate, sometimes with gland-tipped teeth. In foliage the two are also not particularly alike, the oblanceolate leaves of *L. brachycalyx* tapering to the apex whereas those of *L. kelloggii* are spatulate and rounded or even emarginate.

As with nearly all the species there is a certain amount of variation within *L. brachycalyx* and plants grown in recent years from seed introductions by Mrs Sally Walker of Tucson, Arizona are not exactly the same as those which have been cultivated in the past, although both are certainly *L. brachycalyx*.

The species has a southern distribution, in the San Bernadino and Cuyamaca mountains of southern California, and in Arizona where it is recorded in five counties. Tidestrom's *Flora of Utah and Nevada* (1925) gives southern Utah as a dubious record and it is also cited as occurring in New Mexico in several Floras but is not accepted as a native of that State by Martin & Hutchins in *Flora of New Mexico* (1980). In the original description by A. Gray, specimens were cited from 'W New Mexico', although these are probably from Arizona, and from Utah, hence the inclusion of that State in some accounts of the genus. In the apparent absence of any new records it must be assumed that *L. brachycalyx* is restricted to Arizona and southern California where it is a plant of damp mountain meadows and lake sides in open situations between yellow pines, *Pinus ponderosa*. Sonia Lowzow of Arizona has noted that it grows in very sandy situations with rapid drainage, so that little moisture is retained around the fleshy crown of the plant. Although in the spring growing season there is plenty of water available, by early summer the plants dry out and soon there is no sign of growth above ground. However, in late summer and early autumn there is a somewhat rainy season, so that the roots probably never become excessively parched and sunbaked. There is normally snow cover in winter while the plants are dormant, and the minimum temperatures at this time might be in the region of −20°C to −28°C, according to Sonia Lowzow. Clearly there should be no hardiness difficulties over cultivation and any problems experienced in a climate such as that of Britain are likely to be as a result of excessive dampness rather than cold.

Plate 7

Lewisia congdonii

CHRISTABEL KING

Plate 8

Lewisia columbiana subsp. *wallowensis* (left and above)
Lewisia columbiana subsp. *rupicola* (right)   CHRISTABEL KING

Plate 9

Lewisia leeana (bottom)
Lewisia leeana 'Alba' (top)

CHRISTABEL KING

Plate 10

Lewisia cotyledon var. *cotyledon* (bottom)
Wild-collected variants of *Lewisia cotyledon*   CHRISTABEL KING

Lewisia brachycalyx has a relatively long history of cultivation and is recorded as having flowered at the Royal Botanic Gardens, Kew in 1875. A herbarium specimen of this particular plant is in existence, confirming the identity. Little was heard of the species until the 1930s when a very good colour illustration was published in 1936 in *Curtis's Botanical Magazine* (t.7465) and this was followed by a Royal Horticultural Society Award of Merit in 1938. At the present time this most attractive lewisia is rather uncommon in cultivation. Although the name crops up fairly frequently, the plants all too often turn out to be the less showy *L. nevadensis*. This has smaller flowers only 2–3.5 cm in diameter with the bracts separated from the calyx by a pedicel 1–4 cm in length and, as noted by Mrs Margaret Williams (in R.C. Elliott, *Lewisias* 41, 1978), the flowers are usually not rounded but slightly asymmetric; those of *L. brachycalyx* on the other hand are roundish in outline with broad overlapping petals giving a very substantial and regular appearance. Although normally white-flowered, *L. brachycalyx* is recorded as sometimes being pinkish in the wild, and there have been pink forms in cultivation from time to time. Sally Walker of Tucson, Arizona notes that in the populations of *L. brachycalyx* at Show Low, Arizona most of the flowers are white but others are in varying degrees of pink and some have petals striped with pink.

Lewisia brachycalyx Engelm. ex A. Gray in Proc. Amer. Acad. Arts 7: 400 (1868). Types: W New Mexico (?Arizona), *Newberry* (?GH); Arizona, Fort Whipple, *Coues & Palmer* (?GH); Utah, *Brewer* (?GH).

L. brachycarpa S. Watson in Bot. Calif. 1: 79 (1880) — mistake for *L. brachycalyx*.

Oreobroma brachycalyx (Engelm. ex A. Gray) Howell in Erythea 1: 31 (1893).

DESCRIPTION. *Low, near-stemless, deciduous perennial* less than 10 cm in height when in flower with a tuft of many basal leaves produced from a short thick caudex which has fleshy branching roots. *Basal leaves* many, dull slightly glaucous green, oblanceolate, 3–8 cm long, (2–)5–15(–22) mm wide, tapered to an acute or obtuse apex, flat, fleshy, spreading and forming a loose rosette, exceeding the inflorescences. *Inflorescences* consisting of several semi-prostrate to suberect, 1-flowered scapes, 1–6 cm long. *Bracts* 2, sepaloid, opposite, ovate or broadly lanceolate, 5–7 mm long, entire,

63

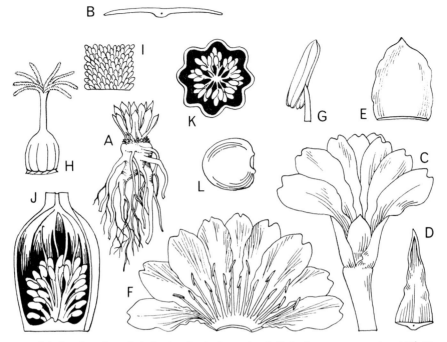

Lewisia brachycalyx. A, habit (resting bud stage), ×⅓; **B**, leaf, transverse section, ×1½; **C**, bud, ×1; **D**, stem-leaf, ×2; **E**, sepal, ×2; **F**, corolla, opened out, ×1; **G**, anther, ×6; **H**, gynoecium, ×2; **I**, part of style-branch, ×20; **J**, ovary, longitudinal section, ×6; **K**, ovary, transverse section, ×6; **L**, seed, ×10.

herbaceous with scarious margins and an angular keel, situated immediately beneath the sepals, the flower thus being sessile. *Flowers* sessile, 3–5(–6) cm in diameter. *Sepals* 2, ovate, 4–9 mm long, acute, entire. *Petals* 5–9, white or occasionally veined with pink, or wholly pinkish, obovate, 12–26 mm long, cuneate at the base, rounded and slightly crenate or emarginate at the apex, sometimes with a thickened blunt apiculus. *Stamens* 10–15. *Style* deeply divided into 5–8 branches. *Capsule* ovoid, 6–9 mm long. *Seeds* 40 or more, black, obovate, 1.5 mm long, shiny.

ILLUSTRATIONS. PLATES 2, 14C, 14D, 14E. Curtis's Bot. Mag. 159: t.9465 (1936); Bull. Alpine Gard. Soc. 56: 65 (1988).

FLOWERING PERIOD. May–June.

HABITAT. Seasonally moist 'alpine meadows', often in open *Pinus ponderosa* woods, usually in sandy soil; altitude 1370–2450 m.

DISTRIBUTION. USA: S California (in the San Bernadino and Cuyamaca Mts.), Arizona (Apache Co., Coconino Co., Gila Co., Navajo Co. and Yavapai Co.), ?S Utah, ?New Mexico. MAP 5, p. 61.

64

6. LEWISIA TRIPHYLLA

This is among the least showy of all the species lewisias with small white or pale pink flowers, and it is thus of no great horticultural value, but in its wild state a well-flowered plant is probably quite attractive. Although lacking in aesthetic appeal it is of considerable interest botanically for it has some unusual features which make it one of the most distinct. The underground parts consist of a small nearly spherical tuber from which arise slender fibrous roots and almost thread-like aerial stems which are clearly very easily broken off from the tuber, for there are very few intact specimens to be found in herbaria! Unlike most of the lewisias which form basal rosettes of leaves, *L. triphylla* produces aerial stems carrying paired or whorled leaves, not necessarily in threes as the name implies. On flowering plants no basal leaves are present but in immature individuals a few narrowly linear leaves arise directly from the tuber. The inflorescence is variable in structure, sometimes umbellate and sometimes paniculate, and the stature of the whole plant varies somewhat from compact dwarfs of a few centimetres to elongated lax specimens 15 cm in height. However, Wayne Roderick tells me that the millions of *L. triphylla* he has seen in the wild have been remarkable for their uniformity. The plant does in fact look far more like a *Claytonia* (especially *C. lanceolata* Pursh with which it sometimes occurs) than a *Lewisia*, and indeed it was as *C. triphylla* that it was originally described in 1875. The structure of the capsule is an important character in the delimitation of the genera in the Portulacaceae and in *L. triphylla* it is circumscissile near the base, in common with other *Lewisia* species; it is therefore best to follow B.L. Robinson (1897) in treating it as a member of this genus, albeit a rather atypical one. The unique combination of characters of *L. triphylla* prompted Rydberg (1906) to place the species in a genus of its own, *Erocallis*, but there appears to be no sound basis for this approach.

Lewisia triphylla is a very widespread species in western North America, from British Columbia and Vancouver Island, south through the Cascade mountains to the Sierra Nevada in California and in the Rocky Mountains from Montana south to Colorado. Herbarium records are, however, not plentiful, probably because of the inconspicuous nature of the plant and its similarity to the slightly larger and much more frequently collected *Claytonia lanceolata*.

Lewisia triphylla (S. Watson) B.L. Robinson in A. Gray, Syn. Fl. N. Amer. 1: 269 (1897). Type: California, 'above Cisco', July 1867, *S. Watson* (lectotype selected by Rydberg in 1932, ?GH).
Claytonia triphylla S. Watson in Proc. Amer. Acad. Arts 10: 345 (1875).
Oreobroma triphyllum (S. Watson) Howell in Erythea 1: 33 (1893).
Erocallis triphylla (S. Watson) Rydberg in Bull. Torrey Bot. Club 33: 140 (1906).

DESCRIPTION. *Deciduous perennial* 2–25 cm in height when in flower, with no basal leaves at flowering time, the slender leafy stems produced from a ± globose tuber 3–10 mm in diameter. *Basal leaves* (on non-flowering plants) narrowly linear, up to 5 cm long. *Stem-leaves* 2–3(–5), subtending the inflorescence, linear, 1–5 cm long, 1.5–2.5 mm wide, obtuse or subacute, opposite or verticillate, margins smooth. *Stems* 1–5 per plant, very slender, especially the underground part, 3–11 cm long. *Inflorescence* subumbellate or paniculate with up to 25 flowers, rarely only 1 or 2. *Bracts* ovate or lanceolate, 1–5 mm long, obtuse or subacute, entire. *Pedicels* slender, 5–15 (–25) mm long. *Flowers* 8–14 mm in diameter. *Sepals* 2, ovate, 2–4 mm long, rounded or obtuse, entire. *Petals* 5–9, white or pinkish, with darker veins, elliptic, elliptic-obovate or elliptic-ovate, 4–7 mm long, 2–2.5 mm wide. *Stamens* (3–)4(–5). *Stigma* divided into 3–5 branches. *Capsule* ovoid, 3–4 mm long. *Seeds* 8–25, dark brown or black, obliquely ovate, *c.* 1 mm long, shiny, shallowly tuberculate.

ILLUSTRATIONS. PLATES 15A, 15B. R.C. Elliott, Lewisias (ed. 2) 69 (1978); R.A. Ross & H.L. Chambers, Wildflowers of the W. Cascades pl. 44 (1988).

FLOWERING PERIOD. May–August.

HABITAT. Open or slightly shaded places in sandy or gravelly soils, sometimes in alpine meadows, usually near melting snow, moist in spring, dryish in summer; altitude 1500–3270 m.

DISTRIBUTION. CANADA: British Columbia (Rocky Mountains & Selkirk Range), Vancouver Island (Crest Mt.). USA: Washington (Cascade and Wenatchee ranges southwards), Oregon (Cascade Mts.), NW Nevada, N California and south through the Sierra Nevada; Rocky Mountains from Montana south through Idaho and Wyoming to Utah, NE Nevada and N Colorado

7. LEWISIA OPPOSITIFOLIA

The reasons for the choice of specific epithet for this species are not altogether clear when the plant is seen in its growing state, because

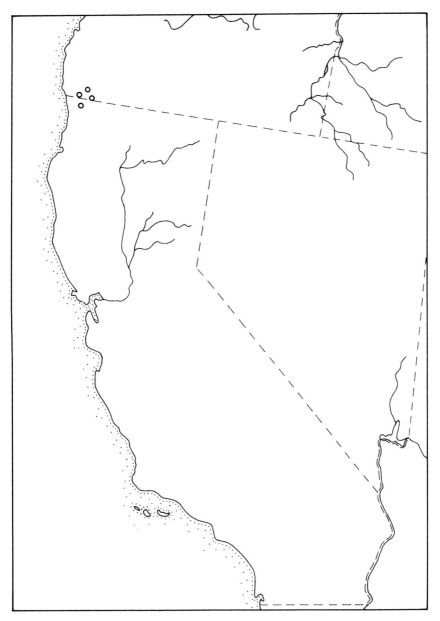

Map 6. Distribution of *Lewisia oppositifolia*.

the stem-leaves, which are well developed, are produced close together and so low down on the stem that they appear to be basal, along with the truly basal leaves. On closer inspection it is, however, quite clear that they are carried in pairs on the stem, making this species a very distinctive one, scarcely requiring comparison with any other. In nearly all the other species the stem-leaves, if any, are much reduced and are more like bracts than proper foliage leaves. The only other *Lewisia* to have well-developed stem-leaves is *L. triphylla* but this is quite distinct from *L. oppositifolia* since it has a different root-stock in the form of a nearly spherical tuber, and the leaves are more often in whorls of three than in pairs. The flowers of *L. triphylla* are only 8–14 mm in diameter whereas those of *L. oppositifolia* are larger (2–3.5 cm across), and the whole plant is of much larger proportions with plenty of other distinguishing features as our illustrations show.

Lewisia oppositifolia is a deciduous species which, like *L. triphylla* and unlike most others, has a fleshy root-stock which is situated well underground so that there is a length of stem, bearing leaves, between the top of the caudex and ground level. Mrs Margaret Williams observes that in the wild 'the leaves are disposed along the underground stem in opposite pairs with only the tips of the leaves coming up above the ground'. Further notes by Mrs Williams in *Lewisias* (Eliott, 1966) concerning the habitat are valuable and it is worth repeating them here. 'This area [Illinois Valley, Josephine Co., Oregon] is at about 1,500 ft elevation and must get about 35 in. of rain annually, and the soil is well drained. Laurence Crocker [the proprietor of the Siskiyou Rare Plant Nursery with Boyd Kline], described the soil as eroded serpentine, and told me that what I thought were bits of gravel, the size of wheat kernels, were iron pellets. He added that the soil is high in nickel and chromium too.'

Lewisia oppositifolia is not one of the most striking species, horticulturally speaking, and although it is clearly rather attractive in its natural mountain habitat it can become somewhat elongated in cultivation and rather less appealing. As can be seen in Plate 3 the flowers are borne on somewhat long pedicels giving a somewhat lanky appearance but in the more compact variant, which is cultivated under the name of 'Richeyi', this habit is less apparent. This dwarf variant appears not to have been formally named and described, although a plant of it was exhibited at the Royal Horticultural Society by G.P. Baker on 18 June 1935 and received a

Preliminary Commendation under the name of *Lewisia richeyi*. *Lewisia oppositifolia* has a long history of cultivation in Britain although it has never been a common plant and is usually confined to specialist collections. It was grown at Kew Gardens in the nineteenth century and was illustrated in *Curtis's Botanical Magazine* of 1889. Sir Joseph Hooker commented that 'the delicacy of its white blossom is its great recommendation to the Horticulturalist. The plants here figured were raised from seed sent from the Harvard Botanical Gardens, which flowered in the Royal Gardens in the summer of last year.'. Undoubtedly it does have a quiet attractiveness and this was recognized much more recently when a plant of the dwarf 'Richeyi' variant shown by Kath Dryden was given the Royal Horticultural Society Award of Merit on 19 May 1970.

As a wild plant, *L. oppositifolia* has a fairly restricted area of distribution in the Siskiyou Mountains of southern Oregon in Josephine County, and in adjacent northern California in Del Norte County. Some field studies are required in order to elucidate the status of the smaller form mentioned above.

Lewisia oppositifolia (S. Watson) B.L. Robinson in A. Gray, Syn. Fl. N. Amer. 1: 268 (1897). Type: Oregon, Waldo, "and in the Coast Mountains of Del Norte County, California, near Smith River", *T. Howell* (?GH).

Calandrinia oppositifolia S. Watson in Proc. Amer. Acad. Arts 20: 355 (1885).

Oreobroma oppositifolium (S. Watson) Howell in Erythea 1: 32 (1893).

DESCRIPTION. *Caulescent deciduous perennial*, 10–20(–25) cm in height, with basal leaves and erect stems bearing opposite stem-leaves, produced from a short underground caudex with fleshy, often branched roots. *Basal leaves* few, green and shiny above, linear-spatulate or linear-oblanceolate, 4–10 cm long, 5–10 mm wide, obtuse or subacute, narrowing gradually at the base to a transparent-winged petiole, the bases underground. *Stem-leaves* similar but smaller, in 1–3 pairs low down on the stem, their bases often below ground level. *Inflorescences* 1–several, bearing loose corymbs or subumbels of (1–)2–5(–6) flowers. *Bracts* lanceolate, 4–8 mm long, scarious, widely spaced on the stem, the upper ones subtending the branches of the inflorescence, entire or dentate at the apex. *Pedicels* slender, 2–7.5 cm long. *Flowers* 2–3 cm in diameter. *Sepals* 2, suborbicular, 4–8(–10) mm long, coarsely dentate with reddish or pinkish teeth, but not glandular. *Petals*

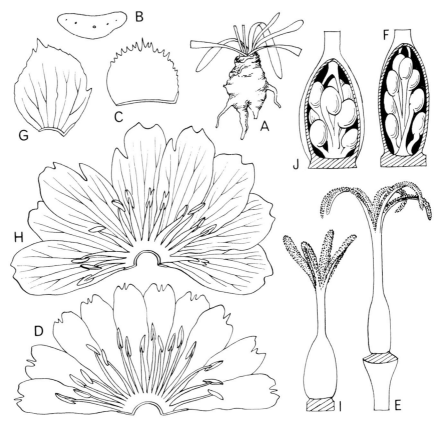

Lewisia oppositifolia. A, habit, ×⅔; **B**, leaf, transverse section, ×3; **C**, sepal, ×4; **D**, corolla, opened out, ×3; **E**, gynoecium, ×6; **F**, ovary with part of the wall removed, ×10.
Lewisia oppositifolia 'Richeyi'. **G**, sepal, ×4; **H**, corolla, opened out, ×3; **I**, gynoecium, ×6; **J**, ovary with part of the wall removed, ×10.

8–11, pink in bud, opening to white or sometimes faintly pink, oblanceolate or obovate, 9–15 mm long, 4–8 mm wide, overlapping, rounded and often dentate or emarginate at the apex. *Stamens* 8–18. *Style* deeply divided into 3–5 branches. *Capsule* ovoid or oblong, 5–6 mm long. *Seeds* 5–15, dark brown or blackish, 1–1.5 mm long, smooth, shiny.

ILLUSTRATION. PLATE 3. Curtis's Bot. Mag. 115: t.7051 (1889) [as *Calandrinia oppositifolia*]; R.C. Elliot, Lewisias 43 (1966); H.W. Rickett, Wild Flowers of the U.S. 5(1): pl. 92 (1971).

FLOWERING PERIOD. March–May.

HABITAT. Rocky and gritty soils, moist in spring, dry in summer; altitude 365–1220 m.

DISTRIBUTION. USA: SW Oregon (Siskiyou Mountains in Josephine Co.); NW California (Del Norte Co.). MAP 6, p. 67.

8. LEWISIA NEVADENSIS

Although *L. nevadensis* has, by some authors, been merged with *L. pygmaea* it is a reasonably distinct entity in this taxonomically tricky genus where there is much variation within species and the delimitation between them is often not clear cut. It can usually be recognized without difficulty by its solitary, fairly large, white flowers, 2–3.5 cm in diameter, with acute or subacute, entire or slightly toothed sepals (there is also a pinkish form, 'Rosea', in cultivation). These features distinguish it from *L. pygmaea* which is a generally smaller plant with white to magenta flowers 2 cm or less in diameter and having the usually truncate sepals dentate or glandular-dentate on their margins. Additionally, *L. nevadensis* has, low down on its unbranched flower-stems, a pair of entire, often green, rather rigid bracts which are 6–18 mm long and frequently curved inwards at their tips, thus partly clasping the pedicel; those of *L. pygmaea* are only (2–)4–10 mm long, often toothed or glandular-dentate and more papery in texture. Taking the length of the pedicel into consideration, that is the portion of flower-stem between the pair of bracts and the flower, we find that in *L. nevadensis* it is 1–4 cm long while in *L. pygmaea*, which often has branched inflorescences with up to seven flowers, the pedicels are only 2–5 mm long, rarely up to 1 cm.

Lewisia nevadensis is a widespread species in the western USA, distributed from southern California north to Washington and east to Montana and Nevada. Not surprisingly, over this vast area there is a considerable amount of morphological variation and it is possible to have combinations of characters which result in rather different-looking plants. For example, forms with rather broad (to 4 mm wide) oblanceolate leaves and short flower-stems can appear very different from those with narrower leaves and long flower-stems. However, there appears to be a more or less continuous range of intermediates and it seems to be impossible to recognize any distinct entities within this species.

As a horticultural subject *L. nevadensis* is not a showy plant and the flowers usually have a slightly misshapen appearance caused by the petals being of unequal sizes. Mrs Margaret Williams has commented that they appear to be 'lop-sided, as though someone had pinched the calyx between his thumb and forefinger, or inadvertently stepped on the flowers'.

71

In the wild it is a plant of gravelly or sandy, usually wettish, places in the mountains, sometimes in the more thinly grassy areas of moist meadows.

Lewisia nevadensis (A. Gray) B.L. Robinson in A. Gray, Syn. Fl. N. Amer. 1: 268 (1897). Type: Nevada & Utah, subalpine region of Wahsatch and East Humboldt Mountains, *S. Watson*; California, Sierra Nevada, 'at Summit and Cisco', *Kellogg & Bolander* (K).

Calandrinia nevadensis A. Gray in Proc. Amer. Acad. Arts 8: 623 (1873).

Oreobroma nevadense (A. Gray) Howell in Erythea 1: 33 (1893).

L. bernardina A. Davidson in Bull. S. Calif. Acad. Sci. 20: 51 (1921). Type: California, Bear Valley, San Bernadino Mountains (specimen not traced).

Oreobroma bernardinum (A. Davidson) Rydberg in N. Amer. Fl. 21: 325 (1932).

L. pygmaea var. *nevadensis* (A. Gray) Fosberg in Amer. Midl. Naturalist 27: 256 (1942).

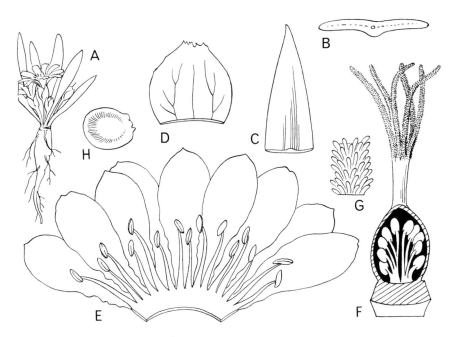

Lewisia nevadensis. A, habit, ×½; **B**, leaf, transverse section, ×4; **C**, bract, ×4; **D**, sepal, ×4; **E**, corolla, opened out, ×3; **F**, gynoecium with part of ovary wall removed, ×6; **G**, part of style-branch, ×30; **H**, seed, ×10.

DESCRIPTION. *Near-stemless, deciduous perennial* up to 15 cm in height when in flower with loose tufts of suberect leaves from a short caudex and conical or almost globose, often branched, fleshy taproot. *Basal leaves* narrowly linear or linear-oblanceolate, 4–15 cm long, 2–6 mm wide, obtuse or subacute, fleshy, usually exceeding the inflorescences. *Inflorescences* of several stout 1-flowered scapes, the lower part of the peduncles subterranean but with up to 10 cm above ground, suberect at first but usually becoming horizontal or deflexed with age. *Bracts* 2, green, or scarious at the margins, opposite, linear-lanceolate, 6–18 mm long, entire, acute, basally connate, often curved inwards to clasp the pedicel. *Pedicels* stout, 1–4 cm long. *Flowers* 2–3.5 cm in diameter. *Sepals* 2, broadly ovate, 5–13 mm long, usually acute or subacute, entire or with a few shallow non-glandular teeth. *Petals* 5–10, white or rarely pinkish, elliptic or oblanceolate, 10–15(–20) mm long, *c.* 4 mm wide, rounded or apiculate, variable in size in the same flower. *Stamens* 6–15. *Style* divided into 3–6 branches. *Capsule* ovoid, 5–10 mm long. *Seeds* many, suborbicular, black, *c.* 1.3 mm long, shiny, muricate.

ILLUSTRATIONS. PLATES 4, 17A. R.C. Elliott, Lewisias (ed. 2) 38 (1966); H.W. Rickett, Wild Flowers of the U.S. 5(1): pl. 92 (1971).

FLOWERING PERIOD. May–August.

HABITAT. Damp sandy or gravelly places, wet grassy slopes and meadows near springs.

DISTRIBUTION. USA: Washington, Oregon, California, Nevada, New Mexico, W Colorado, ?Idaho, ?Wyoming, ?Utah, ?Arizona. The exact distribution is difficult to ascertain.

9. LEWISIA LONGIPETALA

For at least 30 years this species was cultivated, certainly in Britain, under the name of *L. pygmaea* and even when it was realized that the plant really bore only a slight resemblance to that species it continued to be known as '*L. pygmaea* of gardens'. In fact, *L. longipetala* had been described long before, as an *Oreobroma*, in 1913 from herbarium material gathered in 1875 by J.G. Lemmon near Truckee in the Sierra Nevada, California. No further collections were recorded, as far as can be ascertained, until 1968 when Professor G. Ledyard Stebbins discovered a colony in Eldorado County to the south of the type location. It is curious that this species should have become relatively well known in horticulture whilst almost unknown in the wild for nearly 100 years. In view of the paucity of knowledge about *L. longipetala* it is worth quoting (from Elliott, 1966) the story of its rediscovery; in this account it is referred to as *L. pygmaea* subsp.

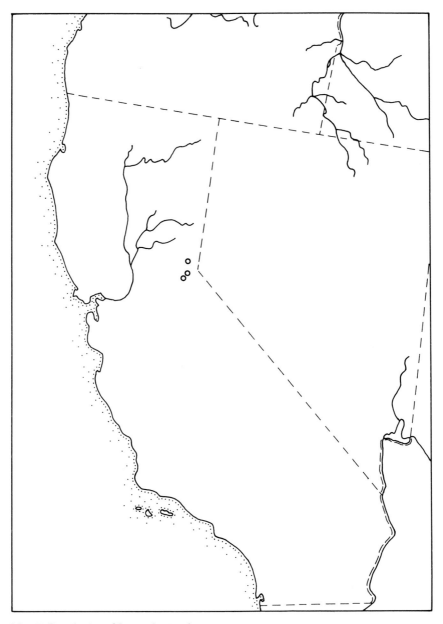

Map 7. Distribution of *Lewisia longipetala*.

longipetala. Professor Stebbins was 'hunting in the Crystal Range, Eldorado County, in July 1968 when he came upon a Lewisia growing at a height of 2600 m (8600 ft) whose pale pink flowers were much larger than might be expected for the two Sierran species, *LL. pygmaea* and *nevadensis*, which were widespread in that area. He identified it as the long-lost *longipetala*. Some days later he found it again, and here lies the particular interest; it was growing within 60 cm of *L. pygmaea* ssp. *pygmaea* and yet was behaving everywhere as a good, sharply distinct, species; there was no hybridizing between the two plants. The larger flowers of *L.p.* ssp. *longipetala* always had one—and only one—flower on each peduncle, whereas *L.p.* ssp. *pygmaea* usually bore two or three. The root-systems, too, were different, for those of ssp. *pygmaea* were relatively short, and tapered strongly—turnip-like—at the base, whereas those of ssp. *longipetala* reached far down into the crevices in which they were growing, were often branched, and tapered little.'. The taproot is indeed capable of reaching to some depth, for one of Prof. Stebbins's specimens in the herbarium of the California Academy of Sciences shows a root which is broken off at a length of 29 cm!

It should be noted that although Professor Stebbins remarked upon the solitary flowers on the specimens he saw, the original description of the species by Piper indicates that the stems can have one to three branches and in fact one of the herbarium specimens collected by Stebbins (No. 6769) does have at least one peduncle which bears two flowers. Certainly in cultivation it not infrequently has branched inflorescences.

There is a striking difference in flower size between *L. longipetala* and *L. pygmaea*, those of the former being up to 4 cm in diameter and not less than 2.5 cm, while those of *L. pygmaea* do not exceed 2 cm. The sepals of *L. longipetala* are also larger than those of *L. pygmaea* and are stained with dark purple, as are the very prominent marginal gland-tipped teeth which, although sometimes present on the sepals of *L. pygmaea*, are small and not very conspicuous. The whole impression of *L. longipetala* is of a larger, more robust plant than *L. pygmaea*. It would seem that, as with *L. sierrae*, this appears to be a rather distinct entity, distributed in a small area within the much larger range of its relatives, *L. pygmaea* and *L. nevadensis*.

The long-cultivated pinkish form of *L. longipetala* is still to be seen fairly frequently in specialist alpine collections, and a near-white form has also been introduced. The neat habit and large flowers

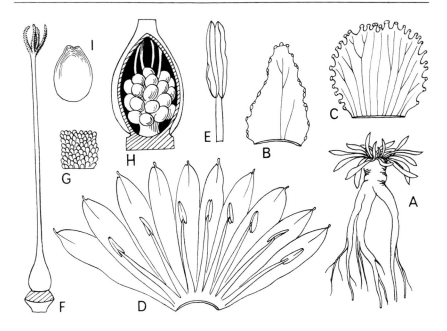

Lewisia longipetala. A, habit, ×½; **B**, bract, ×4; **C**, sepal, ×4; **D**, corolla, opened out, ×2; **E**, anther, ×8; **F**, gynoecium, ×4; **G**, part of style-branch, ×32; **H**, ovary with part of the wall removed, ×12; **I**, seed, ×10.

makes it a suitable subject for hybridization and a few excellent *Lewisia* hybrids have been raised using this species as one of the parents.

Lewisia longipetala (Piper) S. Clay, Present Day Rock Garden 341 (1937). Type: California, Sierra Nevada, 1875, *J.G. Lemmon*, U.S. National Herbarium No. 10881 (US).

Oreobroma longipetalum Piper in Contr. U.S. Natl. Herb. 16: 207 (1913).

L. pygmaea subsp. *longipetala* (Piper) Ferris in Abrams, Ill. Fl. Pacific States 2: 134 (1944).

DESCRIPTION. *Low, stemless, deciduous perennial* less than 10 cm in height when in flower, with a tuft of basal leaves produced from a short caudex with long fleshy branched roots. *Basal leaves* many, mid-green, not glaucous, narrowly linear or linear-oblanceolate, 2–5 cm long, 2–5 mm wide, acute, scarious at the base, fleshy, flat and slightly channelled on the upper surface, convex beneath, forming loose tufts rather than well-defined rosettes. *Inflorescences* consisting of several scapes 3–6 cm long, each bearing 1–3 flowers. *Bracts* lanceolate, *c.* 5 mm long, with conspicuous purplish glandular teeth, the lower 2 opposite, the upper alternate, subtending the branches (if more than 1 flower) of the inflorescence. *Pedicels* rather stout, 1–2.5 cm long. *Flowers* 2.5–3.5(–4) cm in diameter. *Sepals* 2, dark purple, broadly obovate, 4–10 mm long, truncate or rounded at the apex, conspicuously glandular-dentate. *Petals* 5–10, very pale pink ('rose' according to original description) or white, narrowly elliptic-oblong, 11–20 mm long, acute or apiculate, often with a reddish gland at the apex. *Stamens* 7–9. *Style* deeply divided into 5 or 6 branches. *Capsule* broadly ellipsoid, *c.* 8 mm long. *Seeds* numerous, brown, ovoid, *c.* 1.5 mm long, shiny.

ILLUSTRATION. PLATE 5. R.C. Elliott, Lewisias 49 (1966) [as *L. pygmaea* hort.].

FLOWERING PERIOD. July.

HABITAT. Rock crevices; altitude 2600 m.

DISTRIBUTION. USA: California (northern Sierra Nevada, in the border area between Nevada and Placer Cos. (Truckee) and Eldorado Co. in the Crystal Range). MAP 7, p. 74.

10. LEWISIA SIERRAE

This diminutive *Lewisia* is a member of the complex which includes *L. pygmaea* and *L. nevadensis*, where the specific limits are not easily defined. On the basis of the fairly extensive herbarium material available it is apparent that some differences between it and *L. pygmaea* do exist and it would serve no useful purpose to lose sight of what is certainly a recognizable entity by 'sinking' it into *L. pygmaea*. As mentioned under *L. pygmaea*, detailed field study is required to show whether this complex is capable of being fragmented satisfactorily or is in reality better treated as one variable species.

When trying to distinguish *L. sierrae* the size of the flowers is initially the most obvious point of difference, for in this tiny species they are only about 1 cm in diameter when fully open as opposed to the 1.5–2 cm of *L. pygmaea* and 2–3.5 cm of *L. nevadensis*. There are also some features of the sepals which are worthy of note, particularly the absence or presence of gland-tipped teeth and the prominence or otherwise of the veining, although these features do appear to vary considerably and their validity requires further checking in

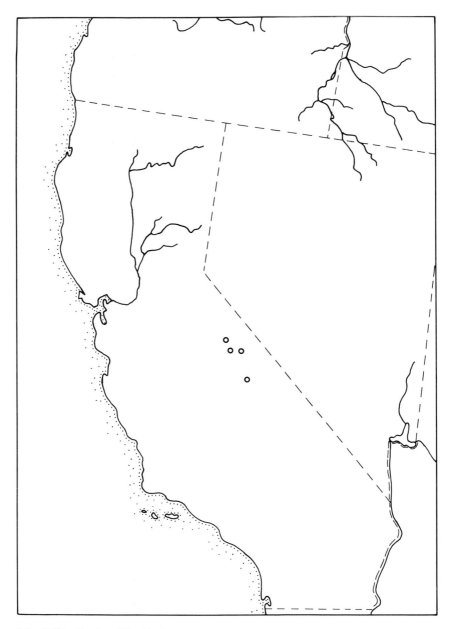

Map 8. Distribution of *Lewisia sierrae*.

Plate 11

Lewisia cotyledon var. *heckneri* (left)
Lewisia cotyledon 'Rose Splendour' (top right)
Lewisia cotyledon var. *howellii* (bottom right)

CHRISTABEL KING

Plate 12

Lewisia tweedyi (bottom)
Lewisia tweedyi, white-flowered variant (top)

CHRISTABEL KING

the field. In *L. sierrae* the sepals are entire, or they may have a few uneven teeth which are non-glandular, and they are more or less smooth without raised veins, although the veins may be conspicuous by being darker in colour. *Lewisia pygmaea* on the other hand usually has sepals with a dentate margin, the teeth are often gland-tipped, and the conspicuous veins become prominent with age, especially as the sepals dry out. *Lewisia nevadensis*, which is clearly distinguishable by its larger white flowers, has sepals with an entire margin or with a few shallow, non-glandular teeth.

Both *L. pygmaea* and *L. nevadensis* are very widespread in the western United States, whereas *L. sierrae* is confined to the central part of the Sierra Nevada range in California where it may some-times be found growing in association with the other two species, and with *L. triphylla*. On the question of identity and distinctness it is often valuable to have comments made about the plants as they occur in their native situations, and especially by astute observers such as Mrs Margaret Williams of Nevada. In *Lewisias* (Elliott, 1966) she comments that in the Yosemite National Park it grows 'in great abundance in the company of *L. pygmaea, nevadensis* and *triphylla*', a remark which surely would not have been made if the variations from one extreme to another were continuous, indicating one variable species. Another experienced field botanist, Wayne Roderick, is of the same opinion and remarks (pers. comm.) that on the basis of all the *L. pygmaea* and *L. sierrae* he has seen, the former tends to have fewer leaves and a few flowers while *L. sierrae* has lots of leaves and many tiny flowers, half the size of those of *L. pygmaea*. He comments also that *L. nevadensis* 'is always *L. nevadensis*' and not easily mistaken for either of the other two. Field notes accompanying a specimen of *L. pygmaea* prepared by no less a botanist than Peter H. Raven observe that it was growing 'with *L. sierrae*, no intermediates observed', a further indication that, to an experienced eye, more than one taxon is involved here. Although I have certain reser-vations about the treatment of *L. sierrae, L. pygmaea* and *L. nevadensis* as separate species, it would be undesirable without more evidence to alter their status or unite them into one variable species.

As a garden plant, *L. sierrae* obviously falls short of being aestheti-cally interesting because of its small size. However, a well-flowered plant grown in the sheltered environment of an alpine house, where it is easily viewed, is not unattractive.

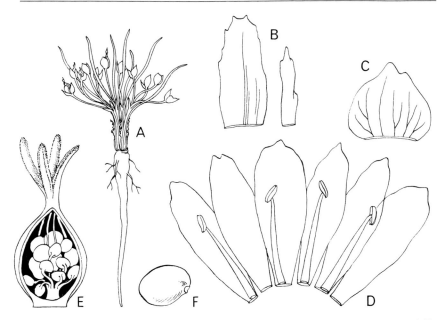

Lewisia sierrae. A, habit, ×1; **B**, bracts, ×8; **C**, sepal, ×6; **D**, corolla, opened out, ×6; **E**, gynoecium with part of ovary wall removed, ×12; **F**, seed, ×16.

Lewisia sierrae Ferris in Abrams, Ill. Fl. Pacific States 2: 134 (1944). Type: California, Sierra Nevada, Fresno Co., Martha Lake, headwaters of South Fork of the San Joaquin River, 5 Aug. 1935, 10900 ft, *Ferris & Lorraine* 9165, Dudley Herb. No. 234110 (holotype DS).

DESCRIPTION. *Low deciduous perennial*, ± stemless, less than 5 cm in height when in flower with loose rosettes of suberect and spreading leaves from a short caudex and fleshy, fusiform roots. *Basal leaves* several, dark green, narrowly linear, 2.5–6 cm long, 1–3 mm wide, fleshy, flat, obtuse or subacute, widening at the base to a winged scarious petiole, forming loose tufts rather than symmetrical rosettes. *Inflorescences* consisting of several radiating procumbent scapes 1.3–2.5 cm long, each carrying 1–3 flowers. *Bracts* usually 2, scarious, sometimes reddish-tinged, opposite or subopposite, narrowly lanceolate to broadly ovate, 3–5 mm long, entire or shallowly repand-dentate. *Pedicels* fairly stout, 1.5–7 mm long. *Flowers* 9–11 mm in diameter. *Sepals* 2, suborbicular, 2.5–3 mm long, 2–3 mm wide, entire or obscurely repand-dentate, usually reddish-veined but the veins not raised. *Petals c.* 6, white or pale to deep pinkish carmine, veined darker, obovate or elliptic, 3.5–5 mm long, obtuse or subacute, unequal in the same flower.

80

Stamens 5–7. *Style* divided into 3 or 4 branches. *Capsule* ovoid, 2.5–3 mm long. *Seeds* 18–20, blackish, 0.5 mm long, shiny, minutely rugose.

ILLUSTRATION. PLATE 6. R.C. Elliott, Lewisias (ed. 2) 60 (1978).

FLOWERING PERIOD. July–August(–September).

HABITAT. Open sandy and gravelly places and in short turf, seasonally moist; altitude 2375–4115 m.

DISTRIBUTION. USA: California (central Sierra Nevada from Tuolumne Co. south to Tulare Co.). MAP 8, p. 78.

11. LEWISIA PYGMAEA

This species presents us with perhaps one of the most tricky taxonomic problems in the genus *Lewisia* for it is extremely widespread and variable and there is no apparent pattern to the variation. Indeed, Hitchcock *et al.*, in *Vascular plants of the Pacific Northwest* (1964), merged *L. nevadensis* with *L. pygmaea* with the comment that 'recognition of even the two following taxa [i.e. var. *pygmaea* and var. *nevadensis*), although they usually are treated as separate species, perhaps results in overly accentuating the significance of two extreme phases'. I am reluctant to go to these lengths since with such a wide view of *L. pygmaea*, incorporating *L. nevadensis*, there would be no case for upholding other species such as *L. sierrae* and *L. longipetala*, resulting in an even more unwieldy aggregate and serving no useful purpose for the botanist or horticulturist. *Lewisia nevadensis* is fairly uniform in its features and can be recognized without difficulty by its solitary, relatively large, white flowers 2–3.5 cm in diameter which have entire, acute or subacute, non-glandular sepals. *Lewisia pygmaea* on the other hand varies greatly and can have one to seven, white or pink to rich magenta flowers 1.5–2 cm in diameter, which usually have truncate or rounded sepals with dentate margins, often with glands on the teeth.

Not surprisingly, with the wide distribution and high degree of variation exhibited by this species, *L. pygmaea* has been described several times under different names, and it is worth noting some of the more important synonyms. It should be mentioned that *Calandrinia grayi* (1890) was published by N.L. Britton, not as a different species but as a new name for *C. pygmaea* A. Gray (1873) since there had been an earlier usage of the epithet *pygmaea* in the genus *Calandrinia* by F. Mueller in 1858 for an Australian species. Naturally the use of the same epithet for two different species in one genus is undesirable and is not allowable under the International Rules of Nomenclature. However, the fact that the American species has been shown to be a *Lewisia* allows it to revert to the original epithet, *pygmaea*, in the genus *Lewisia*.

Lewisia aridorum (Bartlett) S. Clay, described initially as a variety of *L. pygmaea* from Mt. Adams (Mt. Paddo), Washington, is so named because of the dry bare habitat in which it was growing. Its distinguishing characteristics were thought to be the presence of dark glands on the sepals and glandular teeth at the tips of the petals. It was noted by H.H. Bartlett that it grew intermingled with the typical form of the species which was more abundant in damp or wet sandy places; it seems to me, however, very likely that the production of glands may be encouraged by drier habitats and is not consistent. Some variants of *L. pygmaea* have petals which are entire, and the almost acute sepals are only slightly uneven-dentate, not glandular, so in these forms it does approach the larger-flowered *L. nevadensis*. *Lewisia minima* represents such a variant, described (as an *Oreobroma*) from the Yellowstone National Park in Wyoming.

One of the more distinct variants is that described by Rydberg as *Oreobroma glandulosum* (*L. pygmaea* subsp. *glandulosa* (Rydberg) Ferris) from Mt. Dana in California, in which the bracts and sepals have dark glands which are stalked; thus this is an extremely glandular form, as is *L. aridorum*. One individual specimen I have seen of these glandular variants had the leaves furnished with regularly spaced glandular, almost hair-like, teeth. The anthers of this particular plant were pinkish purple, a feature noted by Mrs Margaret Williams (Elliott, 1966, 51) as being a characteristic of the plants she saw on Mt. Dana. From comments made by Mrs Williams it is clear that within the populations of this glandular variant there is considerable variation in flower colour and leaf width and in the degree of glandular toothing, sometimes with glands on the petals as well as the sepals. One wonders in fact if there is some hybridization taking place in this area between *L. pygmaea* and the nearly related and very glandular *L. longipetala* which occupies an area of the Sierra Nevada just to the north of this region. This is a larger plant than *L. pygmaea* with flowers 2.5–4 cm in diameter, and the purple-stained glandular teeth on the sepals are a very prominent and conspicuous feature. In overall appearance it can be said that *L. longipetala* is much more robust with wider leaves and has more erect inflorescences than *L. pygmaea*, in which the flower-stems are often prostrate or arched over to the ground. *Lewisia longipetala* is, as far as is known, confined to an area of the northern Sierra Nevada where it has been found on only a few occasions.

Apart from the already mentioned *L. nevadensis* and *L. longipetala*, consideration must be given to two other entities in this complex which have been described as species, namely *L. sierrae* Ferris and *L. stebbinsii* Gankin & Hildreth. *Lewisia sierrae* is a minuscule plant, described from the Sierra Nevada, which has flowers only about 1 cm or less in diameter, and sepals which are entire or furnished with a few uneven non-glandular teeth, whereas *L. pygmaea*, as mentioned above, has flowers 1.5–2 cm in diameter with the sepals usually dentate and often glandular; further discussion will be found under *L. sierrae* (p. 79).

Lewisia stebbinsii was described less than 20 years ago from the North Coast Ranges of California to the west of the Sacramento River valley, making it geographically discrete from *L. pygmaea*, *L. sierrae* and *L. longipetala* which occur east of the valley as far as the Rockies, and, in the case of *L. pygmaea*, northwards into the Cascades to Vancouver Island and Alaska. In the paper describing *L. stebbinsii* it was suggested that the nearest relatives were *L. cotyledon*, *L. cantelovii*, *L. leeana* and *L. columbiana*, with the observation that they were, contrary to *L. stebbinsii*, evergreen plants. It seems to me, however, that these species are not the most obvious ones with which to compare it and I have chosen *L. pygmaea* as the most likely candidate for kinship; they are both deciduous, have a similar habit of growth with near-procumbent flower-stems and have linear-oblanceolate leaves. The leaves of *L. stebbinsii* are, however, generally wider, 2–11.5(–20) mm (in *L. pygmaea* 1–4 mm) and the longer flowering stems, up to 14 cm, carry three to eleven flowers in a panicle; *L. pygmaea* has stems not more than 7 cm long and these are often one-flowered but sometimes bear up to seven in a panicle. Although the number of stamens is a very variable feature in *Lewisia* it does appear that *L. pygmaea* flowers have consistently less than those of *L. stebbinsii* (4–8 stamens in the former, 10–12 in the latter).

It is clear that thorough field studies are required before the true taxonomic status of all these species and their variants can be ascertained. This is not an easy task in view of the enormous range of distribution of *L. pygmaea* alone, a vast area stretching from Alaska to California and extending eastwards for about 1200 km to Montana and New Mexico. I would suggest therefore that the best course is to regard *L. pygmaea* as a widespread and very variable species with a few fairly readily recognizable but closely related entities which should, at least for the time being, be maintained as distinct species. To reduce their status to subspecies or varieties now would serve no useful function and such a hierarchy would in any case quite probably require further modification after such a study was completed.

From the point of view of the gardener, there is a considerable amount of variation in the aesthetic appeal of the different forms of *L. pygmaea*, ranging from the small, pale, solitary-flowered ones, which are scarcely worth growing, through to those with several larger deep pinkish carmine flowers per stem. Into the latter category comes the plant which was raised from seed introduced by Mrs Sally Walker from Crescent Lake, Gila County, Arizona. This is a fine, albeit diminutive, alpine plant by any standards and has given *L. pygmaea* a rather better horticultural standing, at least in the eyes of British *Lewisia* enthusiasts. It is one of the better forms which is illustrated in PLATE 4.

Lewisia pygmaea (A. Gray) B.L. Robinson in A. Gray, Syn. Fl. N. Amer. 1: 268 (1897). Type: Wyoming, Bridger's Pass 1856, *H. Engelmann* (MO, ?GH).
Talinum pygmaeum A. Gray in Amer. J. Sci. Arts 33: 407 (1862).
Calandrinia pygmaea (A. Gray) A. Gray in Proc. Amer. Acad. Arts 8: 623 (1873), non F. Mueller (1858).
C. grayi Britton in Bull. Torrey Bot. Club 17: 312 (1890). Type as for *L. pygmaea*.
Claytonia grayana Kuntze, Rev. Gen. 1: 57 (1891).
Oreobroma pygmaeum (A. Gray) Howell in Erythea 1: 33 (1893).
O. grayi (Britton) Rydberg in Mem. New York Bot. Gard. 1: 137 (1900).
O. minimum A. Nelson in Bull. Torrey Bot. Club 27: 260 (1900). Type: Wyoming, Yellowstone Nat. Park, Obsidian Creek, 22 July 1899, *A. Nelson* 6076 (holotype RM).
L. pygmaea var. *aridorum* Bartlett in Bot. Gaz. 44: 303 (1907). Type: Washington, Yakima Co., Mt. Adams (Mt. Paddo), *Suksdorf* 5725 (holotype ?WTU; isotypes GH, NA)
L. minima (A. Nelson) A. Nelson in Coulter & Nelson, New Man. Bot. Rocky Mts. 179 (1909).
O. aridorum (Bartlett) A. Heller in Muhlenbergia 6: 83 (1910).

L. exarticulata St. John in Res. Stud. State Coll. Wash. 1: 59 (1929).
Type: Washington, Pierce Co., Mt. Ranier, Panorama Point, *F.A.*
Warren 751 (holotype WTU).

O. exarticulatum (St. John) Rydberg in N. Amer. Fl. 21: 324 (1932).

O. glandulosum Rydberg in N. Amer. Fl. 21: 325 (1932). Type:
California, Sierra Nevada, Mount Dana, 3650 m, July 1902, *Hall*
& Babcock 3611 (holotype NY).

L. pygmaea subsp. *glandulosa* (Rydberg) Ferris in Abrams, Ill. Fl.
Pacific States 2: 134 (1944).

DESCRIPTION. *Low, deciduous perennial*, ± stemless, less than 10 cm in
height when in flower with a tuft of mostly suberect, but sometimes
spreading leaves produced from a short caudex, and a carrot-shaped,
occasionally branched, fleshy taproot. *Basal leaves* several to many, dark
green, linear or linear-oblanceolate, 3–9 cm long, 1–4(–4.5) mm wide,
obtuse or acute, widening at the base into a winged petiole with scarious
margins, usually exceeding the inflorescences and forming loose tufts rather

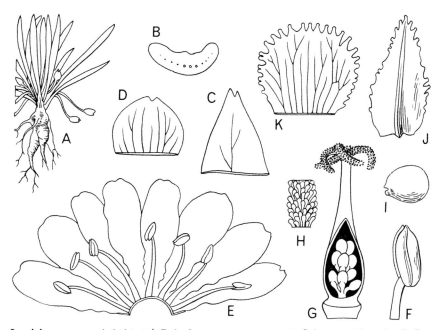

Lewisia pygmaea. A, habit, ×½; **B**, leaf, transverse section, ×4; **C**, bract, ×4 (see also J); **D**,
sepal, ×4 (see also K); **E**, corolla, opened out, ×3; **F**, anther, ×10; **G**, gynoecium with part of
ovary wall removed, ×6; **H**, part of style-branch, ×32; **I**, seed, ×8; **J**, bract, ×6; **K**, sepal, ×6.
Note: **J** and **K** show a typical bract and sepal, with glandular teeth. Occasionally, plants may
have bracts and sepals with few teeth, as in **C** and **D**.

than definite rosettes. *Inflorescences* consisting of several scapes 1–6 cm long, each carrying 1–7 flowers, ± prostrate, or suberect but if so then becoming deflexed in the fruiting stage. *Bracts* linear-oblong, linear-lanceolate or lanceolate, (2–)4–10 mm long, the lower 2 opposite and connate at the base, the upper ones alternate, subtending the branches of the inflorescence (if more than 1 flower), sometimes glandular-dentate. *Pedicels* stout, 2–5(–10) mm long. *Flowers* 1.5–2 cm in diameter. *Sepals* 2, suborbicular, broadly ovate or obovate, 2–6 mm long, usually truncate but sometimes rounded, obtuse, subacute or apiculate, the margins usually dentate or glandular-dentate with the glands sometimes dark purple or brownish, strongly reticulate-veined, especially in the older stages. *Petals* 5–9, white or pink to magenta-purple, sometimes green at the base, narrowly oblong, elliptic or oblanceolate, 6–10 mm long, sometimes glandular-dentate at the apex, unequal in the same flower. *Stamens* (4–)5–8. *Style* deeply divided into 3–6 branches. *Capsule* ovoid, 4–5 mm long, membranous. *Seeds* 15–24, black, ovate to obovate, 1–2 mm long, shiny, minutely muricate.

ILLUSTRATIONS. PLATES 4, 16A. H.W. Rickett, Wild Flowers of the U.S. 5(1): pl. 92 (1971). R.C. Elliott, Lewisias (ed. 2) 49 (bottom plate only), 50 (1978); Bull. Alpine Gard. Soc. 54: 312 (1986); Rocky Mountain Alpines (Amer. Rock Gard. Soc.) pl. 6 (1986).

FLOWERING PERIOD. Late May–August.

HABITAT. Open places in the mountains in short turf or gravelly or rocky situations, moist or dryish at flowering time; altitude 2745–4020 m.

DISTRIBUTION. USA: Alaska, Arizona, California, Colorado, Montana, New Mexico, Oregon, ?Utah, Washington and Wyoming; CANADA: Vancouver Island and the Cascade Mts. of S British Columbia.

12. LEWISIA STEBBINSII

Lewisia stebbinsii was discovered in 1967 by Roman Gankin and W. Richard Hildreth in the North Coast Range of California in the Mendocino National Forest near Bald Mountain, at a place known as Hell's Half Acre because of the piles of volcanic rubble strewn about. The species is named after Professor G. Ledyard Stebbins of the Genetics Department, University of California, Davis, who was President of the Californian Native Plant Society and a co-author in 1974, with L.R. Heckard, of the paper which described *L. serrata*.

Plate 6, prepared from a cultivated specimen, shows the overall facies of the species very well, particularly the conspicuously white-centered flowers. However, the individual used for the illustration has leaves which are rather narrower than is usual for the species: the

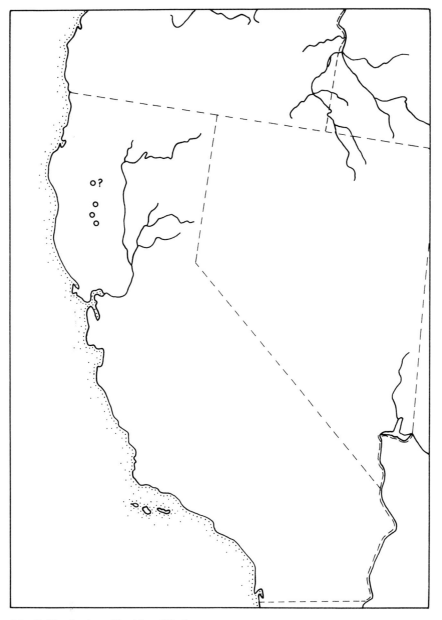

Map 9. Distribution of *Lewisia stebbinsii*.

leaves are normally considerably wider and distinctly oblanceolate or spatulate. Also, in Plate 6, the flowers are a little paler than the usual magenta-rose colour. Additional points of interest about the species are the spreading, branching flower-stems bearing up to eleven flowers, and the long slender pedicels, 8–25 mm in length. In the original paper where the species is described, the authors state that *L. stebbinsii* is 'set aside from all other species in this genus by virtue of its leaf shape, habit of growth (procumbent scapes) and flower colour. The deep rose-coloured outer portion of the corolla and white inner portion is practically unknown in the genus. The leaves are early deciduous, falling from the thickened underground caudex before the flowering stem falls. The flowering stem falls free when the seed becomes ripe leaving, by mid summer, no sign whatsoever of the plant.'. The view is expressed that the affinities of *L. stebbinsii* lie with *L. cotyledon*, *L. columbiana*, *L. leeana* and *L. cantelovii* which are all species with evergreen rosettes. There is curiously no mention of *L. pygmaea* which would appear to be a more likely candidate for close relationship. The latter is a deciduous species often with procumbent scapes which may bear several flowers of a bright magenta-rose, although they are more frequently pale pink or white and are often solitary. A further point worthy of note is that the 'stem-leaves', or bracts, in *L. cotyledon* and its allies are usually alternate whereas the lowest two in *L. pygmaea* and *L. stebbinsii* are normally opposite. The spatulate leaf shape noted above for *L. stebbinsii* is helpful in distinguishing it from *L. pygmaea* and its allies, although the latter can have leaves which are wider towards the tip; the width however is significant, *L. pygmaea* having leaves 1–4 mm wide, while those of *L. stebbinsii* are 3–20 mm wide. Thus, although apparently related, *L. stebbinsii* is a distinct entity, immediately recognizable in the living state from *L. pygmaea* by its generally larger size, larger brightly coloured flowers with a conspicuous white central zone and longer inflorescences which usually carry more flowers on longer pedicels. As far as can be ascertained, *L. pygmaea* does not occur in the North Coast Range of California, having a more easterly distribution, but an allied species, *L. nevadensis*, does. The latter, however, is easily distinguished from *L. stebbinsii* by its one-flowered inflorescences bearing large white flowers with more or less entire, not glandular-toothed sepals.

As a horticultural subject, *L. stebbinsii* is a handsome low-growing species of considerable ornamental value but is at present very rare

88

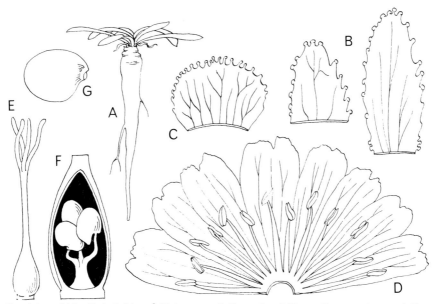

Lewisia stebbinsii. A, habit, ×⅔; **B**, bracts, ×6; **C**, sepal, ×6; **D**, corolla, opened out, ×4; **E**, gynoecium, ×6; **F**, ovary with part of the wall removed, ×16; **G**, seed, ×8.

in cultivation. Although it was only discovered in 1967 it was introduced to cultivation fairly promptly and there is a record of its being exhibited in Britain in the 1970s at an Alpine Garden Society show.

Lewisia stebbinsii Gankin & Hildreth in Four Seasons 2(4): 13 (1968). Type: California, Mendocino Co., '1.3 road miles east of junction of USFS road INO2 on road 20NO2, Hell's Half Acre, ESE of Bald Mountain, Mendocino National Forest' 9 July 1967, *R. Gankin & W.R. Hildreth* 1048 (holotype DAV 40796; isotype DS 621014).

DESCRIPTION. *Low, near-stemless, deciduous perennial* less than 5 cm in height when in flower, with loose rosettes of suberect leaves from a short caudex, and a fleshy few-branched taproot. *Basal leaves* 5–15, oblanceolate, spatulate or obovate, 2.5–8.5 cm long, 3–11.5(–20) mm wide, obtuse, fleshy, shorter than the inflorescences, forming loose rosettes, not well-defined symmetrical ones. *Inflorescences* consisting of procumbent scapes 1.5–14 cm long, branched and each carrying 3–11 flowers in a panicle. *Bracts* glandular-dentate, the lower 2 usually opposite, the upper ones

89

subtending the branches of the inflorescence. *Pedicels* slender, 8–25 mm long. *Flowers c.* 2 cm in diameter. *Sepals* 2, broadly ovate, 3.5–7 mm long, rounded or truncate, glandular-dentate, conspicuously veined in the older stages. *Petals* 7–10, magenta-rose or rose-carmine, veined darker, white at the base, oblanceolate or obovate, 8–10 mm long, 3–5 mm wide, obtuse or rounded. *Stamens* 10–13. *Style* divided into 3 or 4 branches. *Capsule* ovoid, 5–7 mm long. *Seeds* brown, reniform, *c.* 2 mm long, shiny, smooth.

ILLUSTRATIONS. PLATES 6, 16B, C. R.C. Elliott, Lewisias (ed. 2) 78 (1978).

FLOWERING PERIOD. June–July.

HABITAT. Open, south-facing slopes in dryish rocky or gravelly soil in sparse *Pinus jeffreyi* and *Abies magnifica* var. *shastensis* forest; altitude *c.* 1920 m.

DISTRIBUTION. USA: California (S Mendocino Co., Mendocino National Forest). Known in two areas, ESE of Bald Mt., and N of Bald Mt., but not recorded actually from Bald Mt. itself, or from the adjacent Hull Mt. MAP 9, p. 87.

13. LEWISIA CONGDONII

This rather loose straggly lewisia is mainly cultivated for interest's sake, to 'complete the collection', for its large soft leaves, which do not form a tidy rosette, and its small pale flowers on long stems make it an aesthetically fairly mediocre plant.

It was first collected by Joseph Whipple Congdon, an Attorney in San Francisco, on 31 May 1883 in Mariposa County, California, and since then has been recorded in only a few localities showing that it is a fairly restricted but locally common species in the Kings River Gorge in Fresno County, northwards to the Merced River area of Mariposa County on the western slopes of the Sierra Nevada range. Its habitat is on shaded mossy rocky slopes which are wet in spring but hot and dry in summer. The most frequented altitude range appears to be 500–1500 m but there is a record of 2070–2100 m from the Chowchilla Mts., Mariposa County.

There has been some disagreement as to whether the species is deciduous or evergreen but observations of the plants in cultivation show that they definitely lose their leaves during the summer months and produce a new set in autumn, winter or spring depending upon the availability of moisture and on the winter temperatures. Wayne Roderick informs me that on the Merced River the plants may have leaf-rosettes up to 45 cm across but by June all traces are gone. In

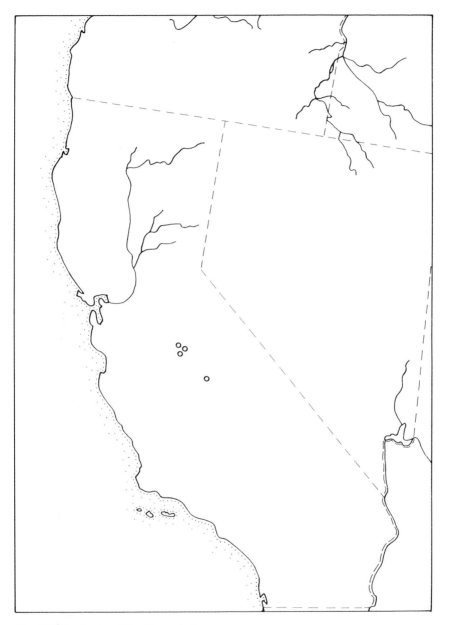

Map 10. Distribution of *Lewisia congdonii*.

spite of this deciduous characteristic the affinities of *L. congdonii* appear to lie with the two evergreen-leaved species, *L. columbiana* and *L. leeana*, whose flowers are very similar to those of the former but rather larger than those of *L. leeana*. In fact, Ferris, in Abrams' *Illustrated Flora of the Pacific States* (1944), regarded *L. congdonii* as a subspecies of *L. columbiana*, but this does seem to be too broad a view and specific status is more appropriate for this rather distinct plant. There are no problems over identification of *L. congdonii*, for the broad, flat, rather thin, soft leaves in loose tufts bear little resemblance to the normally stiff symmetrical rosettes of narrow leaves of *L. columbiana* or to the almost terete (cylindrical) evergreen ones of *L. leeana*. Moreover, the inflorescences of *L. congdonii* are long, up to 60 cm tall, and rather more diffusely branched than in *L. columbiana* or *L. leeana*.

Lewisia congdonii (Rydberg) S. Clay, Present Day Rock Garden 340 (1937). Type: California, Mariposa Co., Hennesey Ranch, 31 May 1883, *Congdon*, Dudley Herb. Stanford Univ. No. 45334 (DS). *Oreobroma congdonii* Rydberg in N. Amer. Fl. 21: 322 (1932).
L. columbiana subsp. *congdonii* (Rydberg) Ferris in Abrams, Ill. Fl. Pacific States 2: 133 (1944).

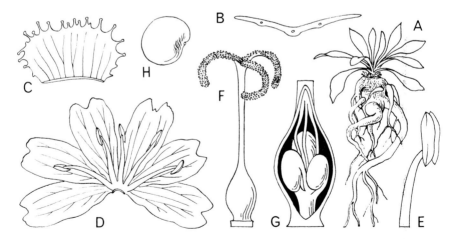

Lewisia congdonii. A, habit, ×⅓; **B**, leaf, transverse section, ×2; **C**, sepal, ×4; **D**, corolla, opened out, ×3; **E**, anther, ×10; **F**, gynoecium, ×6; **G**, ovary with part of the wall removed, ×10; **H**, seed, ×6.

DESCRIPTION. *Deciduous perennial* up to 60 cm in height when in flower with a loose tuft of ± erect (at least in the early stages) leaves from a short caudex which has thick fleshy roots. *Basal leaves* rather pale green, oblanceolate, fleshy but fairly soft and flaccid rather than rigid, flat, 5–20 cm long (including petiole), 10–50 mm wide, acute or subacute, narrowed gradually at the base into a petiole, margin entire. *Inflorescences* of widely branching lax panicles 20–60 cm in height. *Stem-leaves* much reduced, lanceolate or linear-lanceolate, 5–10 mm long, becoming smaller in size upwards, the upper ones bract-like and glandular-dentate. *Bracts* ovate, 2–5 mm long, glandular-dentate. *Pedicels* slender, 5–10 mm long. *Flowers* 1.5–2 cm in diameter. *Sepals* 2, suborbicular or broadly obovate and truncate, 2–4 mm long, glandular-dentate. *Petals* 6–7, pale pink, veined darker purplish red with a yellowish green base, obovate, 7.5–10 mm long, *c.* 5 mm wide, emarginate and toothed to more deeply 2-fid at the apex. *Stamens* 4 or 5. *Style* deeply divided into 3 branches. *Capsule* ovoid, 3–4 mm long. *Seeds* black, *c.* 2 mm long and 1.5 mm wide, shiny.

ILLUSTRATION. PLATE 7. R.C. Elliott, Lewisias (ed. 2) 11 (1978) [photo. of herbarium specimen].

FLOWERING PERIOD. April–June.

HABITAT. In moss in steep rocky slides of shale, and in crevices, wet in early spring, dry in summer; altitude 580–1500(–2100?) m.

DISTRIBUTION. USA: California (Fresno and Mariposa Counties, on the west slopes of the Sierra Nevada). MAP 10, p. 91.

14. LEWISIA COLUMBIANA

Lewisia columbiana was formally described, as a *Calandrinia*, in 1887 by Asa Gray using an epithet suggested but not validated by Thomas Howell. In his paper, Gray compared the new species with *L. leeana*, to which it is undoubtedly very closely related, noting that it could be distinguished 'because of its broader and less terete leaves, not glaucous, and flowering stems less scapiform'. Certainly, the cross-sectional shape of the leaves provides the most obvious difference between the two species, for they are flat on the upper surface in *L. columbiana* and nearly cylindrical in *L. leeana*. In the living state the latter is unmistakable and the tufts of glaucous terete leaves would not look out of place in a collection of cacti and succulents, whereas *L. columbiana* has more obviously defined rosettes of dark green foliage, much more like those of the commonly cultivated and popular *L. cotyledon*, although the individual leaves are much narrower. The inflorescence and flowers of *L. columbiana* and *L. leeana* are quite similar although *L. columbiana* usually has rather larger flowers,

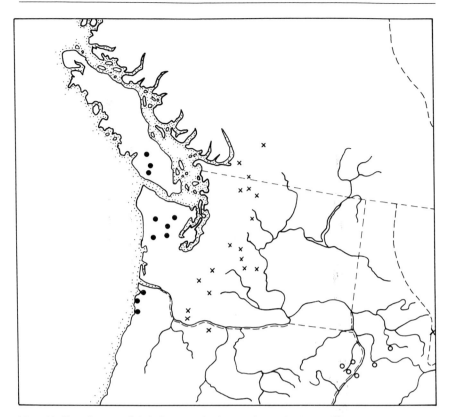

Map 11. Distribution of (×) *Lewisia columbiana* subsp. *columbiana*; (○) subsp. *wallowensis*; (●) subsp. *rupicola*. A newly discovered location further south in Oregon is not shown but is mentioned in the text (see p. 97).

but there is an overlap in size and definitive differences cannot be found here. A study of the distributions shows that *L. leeana* occupies a more southerly range, in California and southern Oregon, whereas the furthest south that *L. columbiana* is to be found is in central and northern Oregon and adjacent Idaho. Reports of *L. columbiana* from further south, in southern Oregon and in California, are almost certainly based on misidentifications. One logical explanation is that these records, or at least some of them, refer to hybrids between *L. leeana* and *L. cotyledon* which, judging by the hybrids which I have seen in cultivation, bear an extraordinary likeness to *L. columbiana*, being intermediate in leaf width between the very narrow-leaved *L. leeana* and the broad-leaved *L. cotyledon*. Certainly these two species do occur in the same region and mixed populations are known; *L.* ×

Plate 13

A, habitat of *L. rediviva* subsp. *rediviva* (open foreground) and *L. tweedyi* (left, sloping woodland), Wenatchee Mts., Washington (photo. B. Mathew); **B**, *L. rediviva* subsp. *rediviva*, east of Ellensberg, Washington (photo T. Walker); **C**, *L. rediviva* subsp. *rediviva*, 4 km NE of Middletown, Lake Co., California (photo. R. B. Burbidge); **D**, *L. rediviva* subsp. *rediviva*, 4 km NE of Middletown, Lake Co., California (photo. R. B. Burbidge); **E**, *L. rediviva* subsp. *rediviva*, white-flowered variant, base of Peavine Hill, Reno, Nevada (photo T. Walker).

Plate 14

A, *L. kelloggii*, Big Valley Bluff, Placer Co., California (photo. W. Roderick); **B**, *L. kelloggii*, Lake Basin, Plumas Co., California (photo. W. Roderick); **C**, *L. brachycalyx*, south of Show Low, Navajo Co., Arizona (photo. T. Walker); **D**, *L. brachycalyx*, location as C (photo. T. Walker); **E**, *L. brachycalyx*, in cultivation (photo. R. B. Burbidge).

whiteae is one such natural hybrid (see p. 138). Some records of *L. columbiana* in California may be referable to *L. congdonii* which is not dissimilar in flower although the leaf-rosettes are considerably different.

The Scottish surgeon and naturalist David Lyall collected what was to become the type specimen of *L. columbiana* during the Royal Navy's British Columbia Boundary Commission expedition of 1860, which was employed to define the boundary between the United States and the British territory to the north. Although Lyall was in overall charge of the plant collections it should be noted that he was aided by a Kew-trained sapper from the Royal Engineers, John Buttle, whom Lyall found to be 'a useful assistant'. The route of the Cascades part of the journey of 1860 was described in some detail by Lyall. Having picked up a trail running in a northerly direction along the Columbia River near Wenatchee, the party followed this until the Okanagan valley was reached which led to Lake Osoyoos. 'Here the party struck off to the north-west up the Similkameen valley, and on arriving at the Ashtnola, a mountain-torrent, ascended the ravine through which it runs, and taking the tributary which led most directly to the southward, got close to the 49th parallel, in long. 120°W.' This indicates fairly clearly that at this point the party was collecting in what is now British Columbia. Lyall lists the plants from the various regions visited (*Journal of the Linnean Society* 7: 124–44, 1863) and for the section devoted to the Cascades and Rockies he notes *Talinum pygmaeum* (syn. *Lewisia pygmaea*) and '*Talinum* n.sp. Cascade Mountains only'. Undoubtedly the latter is that which Gray later named *L. columbiana* and is the collection labelled 'Ashtnola Hills, E side of Cascade Mts. at an elevation of 7000 ft above sea. Found only at one spot amongst rocks. August 1860'; two sheets of this collection are deposited in the Kew herbarium but presumably the specimen from which Gray's description was made is in the Gray Herbarium at Harvard. Interestingly, there is at Kew an earlier specimen of *L. columbiana* from British Columbia which was collected at Campment-des-Femmes', lat. 49°51'N, but there is no indication of who collected it. Exactly how far north into Canada *L. columbiana* occurs is difficult to determine for there are few records available. J. Hohn (1975) cites two specimens from Manning Park in British Columbia, one from 'Hazamann Ridge' (? = Hozameen Range) and one from Lone Goat Mt., both very near to the 49th parallel which defines the international boundary. It is also known from Vancouver Island on several of the peaks including Mt. Arrowsmith.

Together with *L. cotyledon*, *L. columbiana* is one of the most well-known lewisias in cultivation. The form which is most commonly seen in British gardens ('Rosea', or subsp. *rupicola*, see below) produces neat attractive evergreen rosettes of narrow deep green leaves and panicles of many smallish flowers, features which make it aesthetically a first-rate rock garden plant. In its true 'unadulterated' form it is most attractive, but it is also useful for the characters which it imparts to its hybrid offspring. Horticulturally worthwhile hybrids in which *L. columbiana* has played a part include the old *L.* 'Trevosia', with flowers of a warm orange-pink-purple mixture, and the pinkish purple *L.* 'George Henley', both of which appear to have *L. cotyledon* as the other parent, although the latter could possibly be a *L. columbiana* × *L. columbiana* subsp. *rupicola* cross. This hybridization has led to stronger flower colours than are present in wild forms of *L. columbiana*, but the narrow leaves borne in very symmetrical rosettes, which are a feature of these hybrid cultivars, are a valuable contribution from *L. columbiana*.

The concept of the species *L. columbiana* in many gardeners' minds is based upon the frequently cultivated variant known as 'Rosea' which has been around in gardens for several decades, after the 1930s introduction by Carl S. English of Oregon. This is one of the best variants since it has compact deep green rosettes and richly coloured magenta-pink flowers. It has been noted (Elliott, 1978: footnote p. 14) that it is very similar in appearance to the plant described as *L. rupicola* by Carl English jr. in 1934: in fact they appear to be one and the same. *Lewisia rupicola* was collected by English in Clatsop County, Oregon, on Saddle Mt. (*English* 1734) and cultivated by him in Portland, Oregon. The cultivar name 'Rosea' became attached to it and the plant was subsequently distributed under this name; in Britain it was exhibited by Mr W.E.Th. Ingwersen in 1932 with the comment that aesthetically it 'ranks high among the Alpine flora of Oregon'. It is highly probable that most if not all the plants of 'Rosea' in cultivation are derived from this original introduction by Carl English. This cultivar name has persisted in spite of the fact that in 1956 English clarified the relationship between 'Rosea' and *L. rupicola* in an article published in the *Bulletin of the Alpine Garden Society* 24: 27 (1956). He wrote 'I wish to point out that this [i.e. 'Rosea'] is a horticultural name only and that it has no botanical recognition. After due study and observation of this plant in its native habitat as well as in the garden, I considered it a distinct species and so named it *Lewisia rupicola* in 1934.'

A visit to Saddle Mt. with Roy Davidson in 1986 enabled me to observe *L. rupicola* (here treated as *L. columbiana* subsp. *rupicola*) first-hand and I can confirm that the plants growing here are almost, if not completely, identical with those grown in Britain as *L. columbiana* 'Rosea'.

English gave the name *L.* 'Edithae' to a hybrid which he raised, which Roy Davidson informs me is *L. columbiana* × *L. columbiana* subsp. *rupicola*. If 'Rosea' and 'Edithae' are distinct from other variants of *L. columbiana* subsp. *rupicola*, there is no reason why they should not retain their cultivar names within this species. There is, while on the subject of cultivars, a garden-worthy albino variant of *L. columbiana*, known as 'Alba'.

In view of the pattern of variation in *L. columbiana* it seems best to divide the species into three subspecies, with subsp. *rupicola* the westerly-occurring representative from north-west Oregon (where it is only known from Clatsop County), the Olympic Mts. and possibly also the mountains of Vancouver Island. Subsp. *columbiana*, a larger, looser-rosetted plant, is to be found in the Cascade Mts., from southern British Columbia southwards into Washington and northern Oregon. Thomas Howell collected specimens, which he labelled *Calandrinia columbiana*, in 'Oregon, bluffs of the Columbia River near the cascades, June 1886' and these were probably from the south side of the river in Oregon. However, it is possible that Howell was referring to Oregon Territory which had a much wider circumscription than the present State of Oregon. Washington State did not come into being until three years later, so the locality might possibly have been on the north side of the Columbia River. Nevertheless, the species has been located quite a long way south in Oregon in the Cascade Mts. of Douglas County—just one small colony (R. Davidson and S. Hogan, pers. comm.). Roy Davidson informs me that in the Cascade Mts., *L. columbiana* occurs mainly on the drier eastern slopes of the range, which would provide a habitat rather different from the relatively damp western coastal mountains where subsp. *rupicola* occurs. However, *L. columbiana* does also occur on the western side of the Cascades, notably on Mt. Rainier and Goat Mt. (? in Cowlitz County). Although it is difficult to be certain, the specimen which I have seen from the latter locality (*Allen* 205) could well belong to subsp. *rupicola* rather than subsp. *columbiana*, so possibly all the plants of *L. columbiana* occurring to the west of the Cascades watershed belong to subsp. *rupicola*, while all those on the eastern slopes are subsp. *columbiana*; this may, however, be an over-simplistic view and only thorough field study can clarify the situation. Roy Davidson has commented to me that the variant occurring on Mt. Rainier is not exactly like *rupicola*, so it appears that the position is unfortunately not as clear cut as this.

The third subspecies to be recognized (this was suggested by Janet Hohn in her unpublished Ph.D. thesis) is subsp. *wallowensis* which occurs much further to the east, in eastern Oregon, Idaho and possibly western Montana. The westernmost area for this, which includes the type locality, is along the Snake River Canyon in the Wallowa Mts. and it is also on the eastern side of that river in the Seven Devils Mts. in Idaho where Roy Davidson reports seeing 'great cliffsides' of it below Heavensgate Mt.; he has also seen it further east at Gospel Peak on the Clearwater-Salmon divide in central Idaho, and there is a record for western Montana in Ravalli County in the Bitterroot Range, although Roy Davidson tells me that the plants from Montana more closely resemble those from the Cascades, which are *L. columbiana* subsp. *columbiana*.

Subsp. *wallowensis* is variable in the form of its leaf-rosettes which may be almost as neat and symmetrical as those of subsp. *rupicola* or much looser. The individual leaves are usually not as thick and fleshy as those of either of the other subspecies. All the plants which I have seen in cultivation of subsp. *wallowensis* have had pale flowers, almost white, with pink venation, and rather smaller than those of subsp. *rupicola* or subsp. *columbiana*. One plant of subsp. *wallowensis* which was grown at the Royal Botanic Gardens, Kew, produced small, stalked rosettes from the parent rosette in the same way as the reputed hybrid *L.* 'Edithae'; these may be detached for propagation purposes. The latter is almost certainly just a form of subsp. *rupicola* (see above).

Lewisia columbiana (Howell ex A. Gray) B.L. Robinson in A. Gray, Syn. Fl. N. Amer. 1: 269 (1897). Type: 'Mountains of Oregon and Washington Terr., as far north as lat. 49°', *Lyall*. [Possibly represented in herbaria (e.g. K) by specimens collected by *Lyall* in the 'Ashtnola (= Ashnola) Hills, E side of Cascade Mts. at an elevation of 7000ft., August 1860'. This appears to be on the

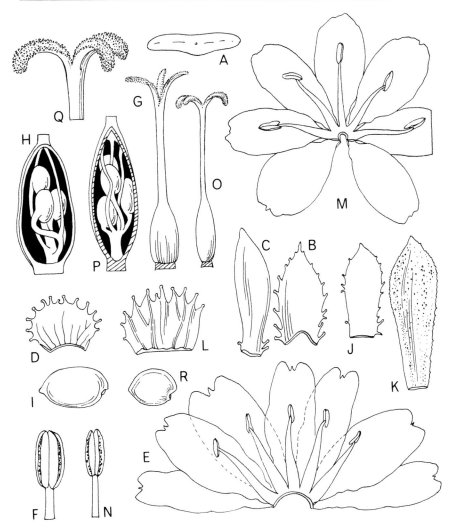

Lewisia columbiana subsp. **columbiana. A**, leaf, transverse section, ×4; **B**, bract, ×4; **C**, bract, ×6; **D**, sepal, ×8; **E**, corolla, opened out, ×4; **F**, anther, ×8; **G**, gynoecium, ×8; **H**, ovary with part of the wall removed, ×16; **I**, seed, ×8. Subsp. **wallowensis. J**, bract, ×6; **K**, bract, ×6; **L**, sepal, ×6; **M**, corolla, opened out, ×4; **N**, anther, ×8; **O**, gynoecium, ×8; **P**, ovary with part of the wall removed, ×16; **Q**, style-branches, ×24; **R**, seed, ×8.

Canadian side of the international border, in British Columbia.]

Calandrinia columbiana Howell ex A. Gray in Proc. Amer. Acad. Arts 22: 277 (1887).

Oreobroma columbiana (Howell ex A. Gray) Howell in Erythea 1: 32 (1893).

DESCRIPTION. *Near-stemless, evergreen perennial* up to 20(–30) cm tall when in flower, with the leaves forming either loose, rather irregular rosettes or compact symmetrical rosettes from a short thick caudex which has fleshy roots. *Basal leaves* many, deep rather dull green, not glaucous, narrowly oblanceolate or nearly linear, 2–10 cm long, 3–8 mm wide, fleshy, flat or slightly channelled on the upper surface, acute, obtuse or nearly rounded at the apex, tapering gradually to the base without an obvious petiole, much shorter than the flower-stems, suberect, forming loose rosettes or spreading to form tight, neat flattish rosettes; margin entire. *Inflorescences* consisting of loose many-flowered panicles 10–12(–30) cm in height with suberect branches. *Stem-leaves* alternate, reduced and bract-like, 5–18 mm long, the lower ± entire, the upper glandular-denticulate. *Bracts* ovate, 1–3 mm long, glandular-denticulate. *Pedicels* 5–13 mm long. *Flowers* 1–2(–2.6) cm in diameter. *Sepals* 2, suborbicular, 1.5–3 mm long, glandular-denticulate, the glands dark red or pinkish. *Petals* 4–9(–11), varying from off-white veined pink to pink or deep pinkish magenta, oblong or obovate, 5–13 mm long, truncate or rounded, often emarginate at the apex. *Stamens* 5 or 6. *Style* deeply divided into 2 or 3 branches. *Capsule* cylindric-ovoid, 3–6 mm long. *Seeds* (1–)3–7, blackish, 1.5–2 mm long, shiny, shallowly warted.

This is a very widespread and variable species with the extreme variants appearing very distinct and worthy of recognition. Since there is some correlation between the distinguishing features and the distribution of the various entities it seems appropriate to recognize them at subspecific level, a course already suggested by Ferris (1944) and Hohn (1975). Inevitably, when dealing with highly variable taxa, one finds individuals which do not conform to the general pattern and almost certainly the key provided below will not 'work' for all specimens of each of the three subspecies; it should thus be used in conjunction with the distribution map of *L. columbiana* which indicates the geographical separation of these variants.

Key to the Subspecies of Lewisia columbiana

1. Leaves obtuse at the apex, ± linear, mostly 2–3 cm long, forming compact flattish symmetrical rosettes; petals mid to deep purple-magenta or rose, (10–)12–13 mm long; bracts, even the lowest, usually dentate and glandular .... c. subsp. **rupicola**
   Leaves obtuse to acute, narrowly oblanceolate, 2–10 cm long, usually forming loose rosettes; petals nearly white with pink veins, or pale pinkish magenta with darker veins, 5–11 mm long; lowest bracts often entire, but if dentate then without glands 2

2. Leaves up to 10 cm long, numerous and thickly fleshy; petals pale to mid pinkish magenta, 7–11 mm long; plants robust, up to 30 cm tall when in flower .... a. subsp. **columbiana**
   Leaves up to 4 cm long, not especially numerous nor thick and fleshy; petals usually white with pink veins, 5–8(–10) mm long; plants mostly 5–15 cm tall when in flower .... b. subsp. **wallowensis**

a. subsp. **columbiana**

ILLUSTRATION. R.C. Elliott, Lewisias (ed. 2) 12 (1978) [top photograph only].

FLOWERING PERIOD. May–August.

HABITAT. Rocky slopes and crevices, recorded on granite, sandstone and serpentine formations; altitude 510–2290 m.

DISTRIBUTION. N AMERICA: Cascade Mts. from southern British Columbia southwards through Washington State, crossing the Columbia River gorge and reaching as far as Douglas Co., Oregon. Possibly also in W Montana. MAP 11, p. 94.

b. subsp. **wallowensis** (C.L. Hitchcock) J.E. Hohn ex B. Mathew, **stat. nov.**

L. columbiana var. *wallowensis* C.L. Hitchcock in Vasc. Pl. Pacific Northwest 2: 232 (1964). Type. Oregon: Wallowa Co., Sacajawea Camp, Snake R. Canyon, 25 July 1950, *Kruckeberg* 2471 (WTU).

L. columbiana subsp. *wallowensis* (C.L. Hitchcock) J. E. Hohn, Biosystematic studies of the genus Lewisia 139 (1975).

ILLUSTRATION. PLATE 8. Bull. Alpine Gard. Soc. 53: 260 (1985).

FLOWERING PERIOD. May–July.

HABITAT. Rocky slopes and crevices, becoming very dry in summer; altitude 1675–2670 m.

DISTRIBUTION. USA: NE Oregon (Wallowa Mts.), Idaho (Seven Devils Mts., Gospel Peak), ?W Montana (Bitterroot Range). The Montana plants may be subsp. *columbiana*. MAP 11, p. 94.

c. subsp. **rupicola** (English) Ferris in Abrams, Ill. Fl. Pacific States 2: 134 (1944). Type. Cultivated specimens from Portland, Oregon, originally collected in Oregon, Clatsop Co., Saddle Mt., 23 July 1931, *English* 1734 ('herb. Carl S. English jr.').

L. rupicola English in Proc. Biol. Soc. Wash. 47: 190 (1934).

L. columbiana var. *rupicola* (English) C.L. Hitchcock, Vasc. Pl. Pacific Northwest 2: 232 (1964).

L. columbiana 'Rosea' of gardens.

ILLUSTRATIONS. PLATES 8, 16D, E. R.C. Elliott, Lewisias (ed. 2) 12 (1978) (bottom photograph, of *L. columbiana* 'Rosea').

FLOWERING PERIOD. May–July.

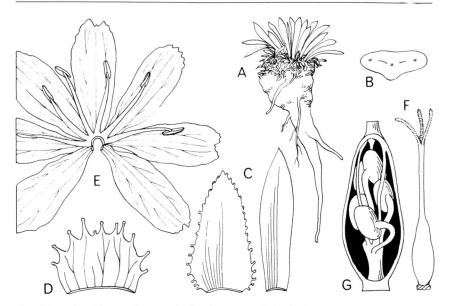

Lewisia columbiana subsp. **rupicola. A**, habit, ×⅔; **B**, leaf, transverse section, ×4; **C**, bracts, ×6; **D**, sepal, ×8; **E**, corolla, opened out, ×3; **F**, gynoecium, ×6; **G**, ovary with part of the wall removed, ×14.

HABITAT. Exposed mountain slopes; altitude 850–1675 m.

DISTRIBUTION. USA: NW Oregon (Clatsop Co., Coast Mts.,—Saddle Mt., Onion Peak, Sugarloaf Mt.), Washington (Olympic Mts., W Cascade Mts., Mt. Rainier, Goat Mt.—possibly subsp. *columbiana*). CANADA: British Columbia (Vancouver Island—Mt. Arrowsmith, Mt. Joan, Mt. Becher). It is not yet confirmed that the plants from Vancouver Island represent subsp. *rupicola* but it does seem most likely. MAP 11, p. 94.

15. LEWISIA LEEANA

Of those *Lewisia* species whose foliage is produced in evergreen rosettes, *L. leeana* is unique in having narrower leaves which are nearly cylindrical in cross-section. It is thus extremely easy to identify in the living state but much less so when reduced to a herbarium specimen, when the flattened foliage could conceivably be mistaken for that of *L. columbiana*. However, the latter has slightly wider, narrowly oblanceolate leaves which are flattish on the upper surface and are carried in more symmetrically formed rosettes than those of *L. leeana*. *Lewisia columbiana* is a more northerly occurring species in British Columbia, Washington, western Idaho and

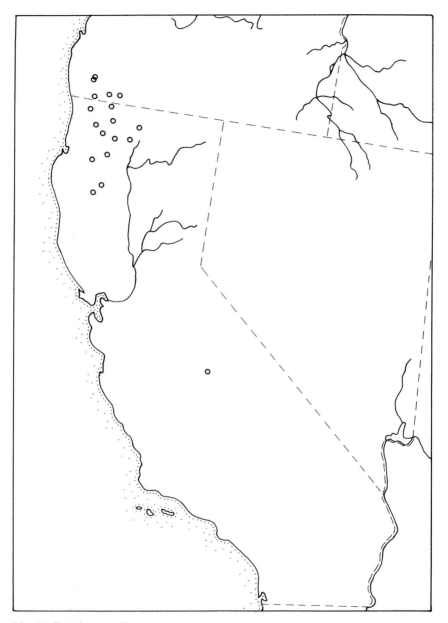

Map 12. Distribution of *Lewisia leeana*.

northern Oregon. *Lewisia leeana*, on the other hand, is found in southern Oregon in the Siskiyou Mountains southwards into northern California as far as the Yolla Bolly Mountains in Tehama County. There are also records from an area some 485 km to the south in Fresno County around the Dinkey Lakes in the Sierra National Forest. It has been suggested that this is a case of mistaken identity but the specimen I have seen (*Kaune* 542) certainly represents *L. leeana*. Dr Janet Hohn (1975) cites another collection (*Bacigalupi* 6725) from the same area, so that the possibility of this being a false record (for example through labels becoming mixed in the herbarium) is extremely unlikely and it must be accepted that *L. leeana* occurs in these two widely separated areas. In the northern part of its range it is widespread and Dr Hohn (1975) notes that 'within the Klamath region [i.e. the vast river-mountain system of northern California], populations of *L. leeana* have been found to occur in every mountain range'.

Although *L. leeana* and *L. columbiana* are clearly distinguishable on their leaf characters it is equally clear that they are closely related, for the inflorescence and floral details are very similar. *Lewisia leeana* is also related to *L. cotyledon* and the two have a similar distribution, although they are morphologically very clearly distinct. When populations meet, hybrids occur and it is interesting to note that these intermediates are sometimes superficially rather like *L. columbiana* in appearance, especially in the narrow leaves which are flattened on the upper surface. The hybrid plants have, however, fairly stout inflorescences and sizeable flowers in a range of bright colours, features derived from *L. cotyledon*, whereas *L. columbiana* has slender inflorescence branches and smallish flowers in white, or pinkish magenta.

Lewisia leeana is named after Lambert Wilmer Lee who made botanical collections in Oregon during a geological survey in the late nineteenth century. The specimen which was designated the type of the new species was gathered on 2 August 1876 in southern Oregon. Although the original spelling of the epithet was *leana* this is incorrect and should be changed to *leeana*, a course which is permissable under the International Rules of Nomenclature.

As a garden plant, *L. leeana* is not spectacular but is nevertheless well worth cultivating for its neat evergreen rosettes and graceful slender inflorescences. There is apparently little variation in the wild and the usual colour is magenta, but albinos occur and have been introduced into cultivation. It is noticeable that the leaves of the white-flowered plants are much more glaucous than those of the coloured forms. Dr Janet Hohn (1975) records that on Baldy Mt. in northern California all the plants in the population of *L. leeana* have white flowers with no trace of pigment and that the leaves of these are very glaucous; the flowers, seeds and pollen also are rather larger than in the other populations which were studied. This white form is in cultivation in Britain as 'Alba' (PLATE 9). On the subject of seeds, it would appear that in *L. leeana* there are normally few in each capsule and Wayne Roderick has found that in the wild the number of seeds produced by each plant is very low. He remarks that in one locality, in Siskiyou County, the specimens were very vigorous with up to 28 leaf-rosettes per plant and measuring 45 cm across, but that the flower colour was a poor pink.

Lewisia eastwoodiana was described by Carl Purdy from specimens gathered in southern Oregon and appears to be synonymous with *L. leeana*. Roy Davidson, who has had the opportunity to study the type specimen, is of the opinion that it represents the white form of *L. leeana* mentioned above.

Lewisia leeana (T. Porter) B.L. Robinson in A. Gray, Syn. Fl. N. Amer. 1: 269 (1897). Type: Oregon, 'Siskyou mountains near the southern boundary of Oregon', 2 Aug. 1876, *L.W. Lee* (location of specimen unknown).
Calandrinia leana T. Porter in Bot. Bull. [later Bot. Gaz. (Crawfordsville)] 1: 49 (1876).
Oreobroma leanum (T. Porter) Howell in Erythea 1: 31 (1893).
L. eastwoodiana Purdy in Leafl. W. Bot. 1: 20 (1932). Type: Oregon, Josephine Co., 'in the region around Waldo and Kirby', *Mary L. White* (CAS).

DESCRIPTION. *Near-stemless, evergreen perennial* 10–20 cm in height when in flower, with the leaves forming loose tufts of ill-defined rosettes from a short thick caudex which has fleshy branching roots. *Basal leaves* many, glaucous, sometimes markedly so, linear and ± terete, 1.5–6 cm long, 2–3.5 mm wide, fleshy, smooth, acute. *Inflorescences* consisting of loose many-flowered panicles 8–20 cm in height with spreading or suberect branches. *Stem-leaves* alternate, narrowly lanceolate, *c.* 5 mm long, much reduced and bract-like, the lowest entire, the upper ones glandular-dentate. *Bracts* ovate to narrowly lanceolate, 2–5 mm long, acute, glandular-denticulate. *Pedicels*

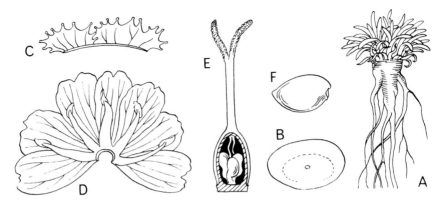

Lewisia leeana. A, habit, ×⅓; **B**, leaf, transverse section, ×4; **C**, sepals, ×6; **D**, corolla, opened out, ×4; **E**, gynoecium with part of the ovary wall removed, ×10; **F**, seed, ×6.

slender, 3–15 mm long, spreading or suberect, becoming arcuate-recurved in fruit. *Flowers* 1–1.4 cm in diameter. *Sepals* 2, suborbicular, 1–4 mm long, glandular-dentate, the glands usually dark purplish. *Petals* 5–8, magenta, pale pinkish purple, white with magenta veining or occasionally white, obovate, 5–7 mm long, cuneate at the base, rounded, retuse or emarginate at the apex. *Stamens* 4–8. *Ovary* containing 2–4 ovules. *Style* deeply divided into 2 branches. *Capsule* ovoid, 4–5 mm long. *Seeds* usually 1 or 2, dark brown, 2–2.5 mm long, shiny.

ILLUSTRATIONS. PLATES 9, 17B, C, D. H.W. Rickett, Wild Flowers of the U.S. 5(1): pl. 91 (1971); R.C. Elliott, Lewisias (ed. 2) 28 (1978).

FLOWERING PERIOD. June–early August.

HABITAT. Open N or NW facing scree slopes and cliffs on granite or serpentine formations; altitude 1350–3350 m.

DISTRIBUTION. USA: California (Del Norte Co., Fresno Co., Humboldt Co., Shasta Co., Siskiyou Co., Tehama Co., Trinity Co.), Oregon (Jackson Co., Josephine Co.). MAP 12, p. 103.

16. LEWISIA CANTELOVII

Lewisia cantelovii was named by J.T. Howell in 1942 in honour of Herbert Clair Cantelow, an American businessman in the Pacific Coast shipping industry who, together with his wife, discovered the species a year earlier in California, on the western side of the Sierra Nevada. It is not a widespread plant and is known from an area about 60 km across, growing on shady vertical cliffs in the canyons of

106

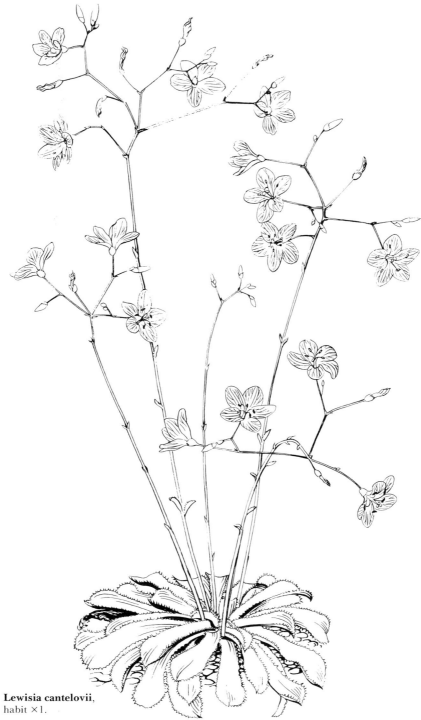

Lewisia cantelovii,
habit ×1.

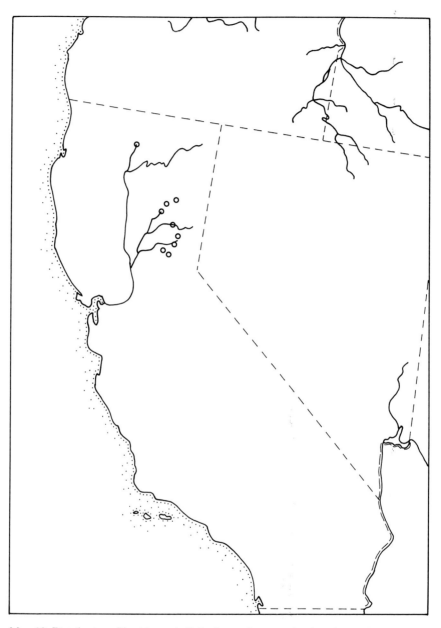

Map 13. Distribution of *Lewisia cantelovii*. In the northernmost locality shown, the plants are not typical of the species and may represent an undescribed infraspecific taxon (S. Hogan, pers. comm.).

the Feather and Yuba river systems. Sean B. Hogan of Sacramento, California has studied the species in the wild and has found that it is somewhat more widespread than was supposed, and shows a fair amount of local variation so that populations from the different canyons can be recognized. It is a distinctive plant, even in its non-flowering stage, for the flattish rosettes consist of many narrow, spatulate leaves which have their margins furnished with very conspicuous sharp, narrowly triangular teeth standing out at right angles to the margin. Furthermore, there is often a purplish suffusion on the underside which reaches the spiny margin giving a slightly pinkish outline to the leaves when viewed from above. The only other lewisias which have prominently toothed leaves are *L. cotyledon* var. *heckneri* and *L. serrata*. The former has few other points of similarity with *L. cantelovii* and the leaves alone serve to distinguish between them. Those of *L. cantelovii* are mostly only 5–12 mm wide whereas those of *L. cotyledon* and its variants are rarely as narrow as 13 mm and usually 2–3 cm wide. Should one require any further distinguishing features there is also a striking difference in flower size and colour, those of *L. cantelovii* being rather pallid, only 1–1.5 cm in diameter, and carried on slender pedicels 5–10 mm long, while those of *L. cotyledon* are much more showy, 2–4 cm across, and are carried on short stout pedicels about 3–5 mm long.

Lewisia serrata is the most closely related species and resembles *L. cantelovii* in its conspicuously toothed leaves. In March 1989 I was fortunate to be shown by Wayne Roderick a population of *L. cantelovii*, in one of the canyons of the Feather River, and also had the opportunity to see the very extensive collection of plants made by Sean Hogan. There was considerably more variation in the type of leaf dentation and shape than I had previously supposed, and it is clear that there is a valid case for regarding *L. serrata* as a subspecies of *L. cantelovii*, a course of action already suggested by Janet Hohn (1975). Pending further studies, however, I have retained them here as separate species. In *L. serrata* the leaves are even more coarsely and irregularly dentate, with the individual teeth more broadly triangular than those of *L. cantelovii*. The most obvious difference in foliage, however, is in the shape; in *L. serrata* the leaves are narrowly obovate and narrowed gradually to the base, whereas in *L. cantelovii* they are most frequently spatulate with an almost orbicular blade narrowing abruptly at first and then tapering more gradually to the base. The apex of the leaf is rounded in *L. serrata* and although it may

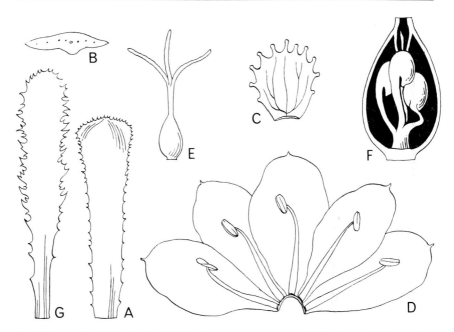

Lewisia cantelovii. A, leaf, ×1; **B**, leaf, transverse section, ×4; **C**, sepal, ×10; **D**, corolla, opened out, ×6; **E**, gynoecium, ×6; **F**, ovary with part of the wall removed, ×20. **Lewisia serrata. G**, leaf, ×1.

also be rounded in *L. cantelovii*, it is more often truncate, emarginate or retuse. In floral characters the two are very similar although the flowers of *L. serrata* are slightly smaller with petals only 5–6 mm long (6–9 mm in *L. cantelovii*). There is unfortunately not a lot of material of these two very restricted species available for comparison but it does appear, as stated by Heckard and Stebbins (1974), that the petals of *L. cantelovii* normally have five to seven longitudinal veins whereas those of *L. serrata* normally have three and only rarely five. However, the comparative number of reduced bract-like 'stem-leaves', which is given as one of the distinguishing features in the same paper, does not seem to be a useful character. The overall length of the inflorescences is worthy of note since in *L. serrata* they usually vary between 10 cm and 20 cm and in *L. cantelovii* they are 15–30 cm, so in most cases the impression is of a more compact inflorescence in *L. serrata*.

Lewisia cantelovii is not one of the most striking of the lewisias but it is a graceful plant suitable for the alpine house, especially attractive

A

B

Plate 15
A, *L. triphylla*, Alex Hole, Siskiyou Co., California (photo. T. Walker); **B**, *L. triphylla*, Castle Lake, Siskiyou Co., California (photo W. Roderick).

Plate 16

A, *L. pygmaea*, Winn Meadows, Navajo Co., Arizona (photo T. Walker); **B**, *L. stebbinsii*, NE of Hull Mt., Mendocino Co., California (photo T. Walker); **C**, *L. stebbinsii*, California (photo. W. Roderick); **D**, habitat of *L. columbiana* subsp. *rupicola*, Saddle Mt., NW Oregon (photo. B. Mathew); **E**, *L. columbiana* subsp. *rupicola*, location as D (photo. B. Mathew).

Plate 17
A, *L. nevadensis*, in cultivation (photo. B. Mathew); **B**, *L. leeana*, Upper Cliff Lake, Siskiyou Co.,
N California (photo. W. Roderick); **C**, *L. leeana*, Castle Lake, Siskiyou Co., California (photo.
W. Roderick); **D**, *L. leeana*, location as B (photo. W. Roderick).

Plate 18
A, *L. cantelovii*, Caribou, Feather River Canyon, Plumas Co., California (photo. W. Roderick);
B, *L. cantelovii*, location as A (photo. W. Roderick).

for its neat symmetrical evergreen rosettes of regularly toothed leaves which are not as gross as those of its flamboyant cousin *L. cotyledon*. However, it is rarely seen in cultivation in Britain, even in specialist collections, although it was introduced at least 22 years ago.

Lewisia cantelovii J.T. Howell in Leafl. W. Bot. 3: 139 (1942). Type: California, Plumas Co., 3.2 miles west of Belden in the Feather River Canyon, 25 May 1941, *H.C. Cantelow* Herb. Calif. Acad. Sci. No. 294735 (CAS).

DESCRIPTION. *Evergreen perennial* up to 30 (rarely 40) cm tall when in flower, with a flattish rosette of basal leaves from a ± globose caudex which has fleshy branching roots. *Basal leaves* dull green suffused with pinkish purple beneath, spatulate, 2–5.5 cm long, 5–17 mm wide, thick and fleshy, flat on the upper surface, with a truncate, emarginate or retuse, or sometimes rounded apex, tapering to the base without an obvious petiole, much shorter than the flower-stems and spreading to form a flattish symmetrical rosette; margins prominently and sharply dentate. *Inflorescences* of several loose, many-flowered panicles 15–30(–40) cm in height. *Peduncles* rather slender and wiry, purplish. *Stem-leaves* much reduced, narrowly oblong or lanceolate, 3–5(–10) mm long, acute, denticulate, the upper ones with glandular teeth. *Bracts* ovate, 1–3 mm long, glandular-denticulate. *Flowers* 1–1.5 cm in diameter. *Pedicels* slender, 0.3–1 cm long. *Sepals* 2, broadly elliptic, 2–3 mm long, *c.* 2 mm broad, glandular-denticulate. *Petals* 5 or 6, white or pale pink veined darker pink, elliptic-ovate or elliptic-obovate, 6–9 mm long, 3–5 mm wide, rounded or slightly toothed at the apex. *Stamens* 5 or 6. *Stigma* deeply divided into 3 branches. *Capsules* ovoid, *c.* 3 mm long. *Seeds c.* 1–3(?), black, *c.* 1.5 mm long, ± smooth.

ILLUSTRATIONS. PLATE 18A, B. H.W. Rickett, Wild Flowers of the U.S. 5(1): pl. 91 (1971). R.C. Elliott, Lewisias (ed. 2) 10 (1978).

FLOWERING PERIOD. Mainly May–June but continuing sporadically until autumn.

HABITAT. Moist vertical rock outcrops with north exposure, or in the shade of trees and shrubs, drying out in summer and autumn; altitude 700–920 m.

DISTRIBUTION. USA: NE California (Plumas Co. and Nevada Co., west slopes of Sierra Nevada in the canyons of the Feather and Yuba rivers). MAP 13, p. 108.

17. LEWISIA SERRATA

This local species which, as far as is known, is confined to a few localities in El Dorado and Placer Counties in eastern California, is one of the few lewisias to have conspicuously serrate leaves. For the purposes of this discussion one of these, *L. cotyledon* var. *heckneri*, can be discounted, for its flowers alone are so different from those of *L. serrata* that an enumeration of the other differences would be superfluous. The only species which really resembles it is *L. cantelovii*, a species occurring just to the north in Plumas and Nevada Counties. These two both have coarsely dentate leaf-margins, although the teeth are not exactly the same and there are subtle differences in leaf shape. An explanation of these and other differences will be found under *L. cantelovii* (p. 109).

There are other species which have similar floral characteristics to *L. serrata*, namely *L. congdonii*, *L. leeana* and *L. columbiana*, but these are distinct in other ways. *L. congdonii* has non-dentate leaves which die away in the summer months whereas those of *L. serrata* remain evergreen; *L. leeana* and *L. columbiana* have evergreen rosettes but the leaves are not toothed, and are nearly terete in the former and flattish in the latter.

Like *L. cantelovii* this is not a showy plant but the characteristically toothed, symmetrical rosettes make it an interesting and distinct lewisia for the alpine house, although it has not proved to be nearly as easy to cultivate as *L. cantelovii*.

Lewisia serrata Heckard & Stebbins in Brittonia 26: 305 (1974). Type: California, El Dorado Co., below Leonardi Springs, S side of Rubicon River canyon, 29 May 1969, *G.L. Stebbins* & *L.R. Heckard* 6908 (holotype JEPS; isotypes DAV, RSA, US, WTU).

DESCRIPTION. *Evergreen perennial* (5–)10–20(–25) cm in height when in flower, with a flattish rosette of basal leaves from a usually short caudex which may sometimes reach 10 cm in length, with fleshy few-branched roots. *Basal leaves* green, narrowly obovate, (2–)4–7(–10) cm long, 10–15(–20) mm wide, fleshy, flattish on the upper surface, rounded, tapering gradually to the base, shorter than the inflorescences and forming a flattish rosette; margins coarsely triangular-dentate. *Inflorescences* of several loose, many-flowered panicles 10–20(–25) cm in height. *Stem-leaves* alternate, much reduced, narrowly oblanceolate, 3–12 mm long, obtuse or acute, coarsely denticulate. *Bracts* alternate or opposite, elliptic or obovate, 1–4

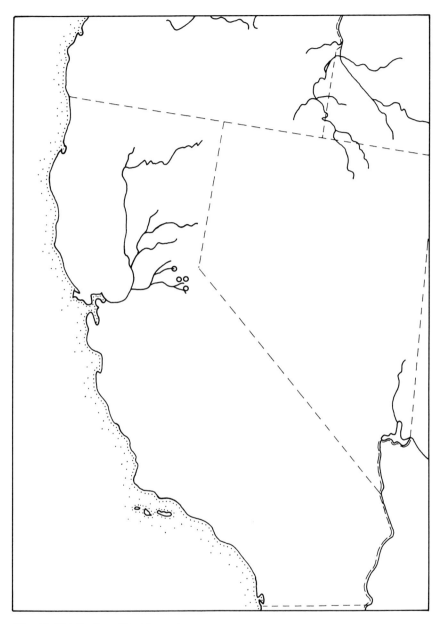

Map 14. Distribution of *Lewisia serrata*.

mm long, glandular-denticulate. *Flowers* c. 1.5 cm in diameter. *Pedicels* slender, 3–8 mm long. *Sepals* 2, suborbicular, c. 2 mm long, glandular-denticulate. *Petals* 5, white or pale pink veined darker reddish pink, elliptic, 5–6 mm long, 2.5–3 mm wide, acute or obtuse. *Stamens* 5. *Stigma* deeply divided into 3 branches. *Capsule* ovoid, c. 3 mm long. *Seeds* 1–3, blackish, 1.2–1.5 mm long, shiny.

ILLUSTRATION. Brittonia 26: 306 (1974). Leaf illustrated on p. 110.

FLOWERING PERIOD. May–July.

HABITAT. North facing shady, moss-covered cliffs and ledges of metamorphic rock; altitude 900–1300 m.

DISTRIBUTION. USA: E California (El Dorado and Placer Counties, in the steep gorges of the American river drainage system). MAP 14, p. 113.

18. LEWISIA COTYLEDON

This attractive evergreen lewisia with its symmetrical rosettes of leaves is the species which most people think of when the genus is mentioned, for it is much the easiest to cultivate and certainly the showiest. The extent of its aesthetic value can be measured by the number of awards by the Royal Horticultural Society both to the species, and to its varieties and cultivars (see p. 142). The species was first described in 1884 from material gathered a year earlier by Thomas Howell in the Siskiyou Mts. in northern California. The date of introduction into British horticulture appears to have been in the early part of the twentieth century; a plant sent in by Mr P.B. Randolph was grown at the Royal Botanic Gardens, Kew in 1906 and this was painted for *Curtis's Botanical Magazine* (t.8220) in 1908. The species was also cultivated by Mr G. Reuthe of Keston in Kent, apparently in about 1907 from seeds sent from the Klondyke area. *Lewisia howellii* (here treated as *L. cotyledon* var. *howellii*) was introduced to Kew in January 1911 by Carl Purdy, and this was followed by other variants such as *heckneri*, *purdyi* and *finchae*, so that by the middle of the century there were several available to gardeners for experimental hybridization.

In the wild, *L. cotyledon* exhibits a great deal of natural variability which has allowed considerable scope for breeding and selection. As a result there are now many horticultural variants in an array of bright colours, as well as hybrids with other species. The natural flower colour is most frequently in the pinkish magenta range, usually pink-striped on a white or creamy ground, but many forms

114

exist from pure white to pink, apricot and yellow, mostly striped rather than uniformly coloured. On the variability of *L. cotyledon* in the wild, Wayne Roderick of Orinda, California has noted that in one of the stations 'the main stand was in shades of pink: pink with red stripes, white with deep pink stripes, cream with pinkish orange stripes, and a few had mauve stripes. One plant I would class as red, while another was nearly white with faint pink lines. The width of the petals, as well as the width of the stripes, was as varied as the shape of the leaves. The foliage varied from near linear to almost orbicular, with some plants having slightly fluted leaves and others having some serration on their leaves.'

This variability of *L. cotyledon* has led inevitably to a degree of 'splitting' and some of the forms have been given distinguishing names. There is, however, considerable disagreement over the interpretation of the variation, and opinions range from those who consider it impossible to recognize any infraspecific taxa at all to the other extreme where several separate species are recognized. Ira N. Gabrielson, author of *Western American Alpines* (1932), made similar observations to those of Wayne Roderick and noted that 'It has been my good fortune to see these Lewisias in their native haunts on many peaks of the Siskiyous and there is a serious question in my mind as to their distinctness. One can go into many colonies and pick out the types of each [referring to *L. cotyledon, L. howellii, L. purdyi, L. heckneri* and *L. finchae*] and also all sorts of intergrades between them. If there are distinct species, they certainly hybridize most freely both in the wild and in cultivation, and for all practical purposes they seem to be variations of one species.'

On the other hand, Janet E. Hohn, in an unpublished Ph.D. thesis (1975), presented the results of a biosystematic study of *L. cotyledon* and suggested that it consisted of five subspecies, subsp. *cotyledon*, subsp. *howellii*, subsp. *heckneri*, subsp. *purdyi*, and a new taxon for which she proposed the name subsp. *fimbriata*. In addition to certain subtle morphological differences these were shown to fall into a distinct geographical pattern.

In view of the widely differing evidence available, I have taken an intermediate view and accepted three of the varieties which have been described in the past, namely var. *cotyledon*, var. *heckneri* and var. *howellii*.

The whole area of distribution of *L. cotyledon* is contained in a region of not more than about 160 km in length and less than 120 km wide and within this area it is restricted to cliff or pavement crevice habitats, mostly above 1200 m although it does descend to 150 m. *Lewisia cotyledon* was first named as a *Calandrinia* in 1885 by Sereno Watson who noted that its 'resemblance in habit to small species of *Cotyledon* [Crassulaceae] suggests the specific name'. This plant represented one of the entire-leaved variants and was found in the upper reaches of the Illinois River in the main chain of the Siskiyou Mountains. *Calandrinia howellii* followed only three years later, again described by Watson, this time from adjacent Oregon, and differing mainly in its narrow leaves with strongly crisped-undulate margins. This has also been found in north-west California, particularly in the Klamath River canyon in Humboldt County. W.L. Jepson, author of *A Flora of California*, added to the list *L. cotyledon* var. *purdyi* in 1914, named after the nurseryman and ardent collector of the Pacific Coast flora, Carl Purdy. This was a broad-leaved form with almost orbicular and rather short leaves, from the Siskiyou Mts. of southern Oregon. I have taken this to be a variant of *L. cotyledon* var. *cotyledon*, insufficiently distinct to warrant taxonomic status, but Janet E. Hohn (1975) suggests that it is consistent in the small size of its leaf-rosettes, and has a slightly different distribution from var. *cotyledon*, in the Kalmiopsis Wilderness area of Josephine and Curry Counties, Oregon. Sean Hogan tells me that he is also of the opinion that this is a fairly distinct variant.

In 1932, *L. finchae* was described by Carl Purdy and named after Mrs J.M. Finch of Kerby (Kirby), Oregon. This marks the upper end of size development in the *L. cotyledon* compiex with large spreading leaves up to 4 cm wide and 6–10 cm long, forming flat rosettes, and with large flowers 3 cm in diameter. Purdy also described at the same time *L. × whiteae* from southern Oregon, named after Mrs Mary L. White of Waldo who collected it in this area of the Siskiyous. This he distinguished as having deep green leaves 6–7 cm long and only 9 mm wide at the apex, and scapes bearing 30 to 40 salmon-rose flowers with seven or eight petals 12–13 mm long, widely spreading to give a flat flower; this is probably a *L. cotyledon* × *L. leeana* hybrid. The third species named by Purdy in 1932, *L. eastwoodiana* (in *Leafl. W. Bot.* 1: 20, 1932), is not so easy to place as a variant of *L. cotyledon* for it was described as having leaves only 8 mm wide and small white flowers with petals 6–8 mm long. In *Lewisias* (Elliott, 1966) this is given as a synonym of *L. columbiana* although it is generally accepted that this species does not occur in the extreme south of Oregon or in California. It seems very likely that *L. eastwoodiana* is a white-flowered variant of *L. leeana*, and Roy Davidson, who has seen the type specimen, has expressed such a view to me.

One of the more distinct variants of *L. cotyledon* was described as *Oreobroma heckneri* by C.V. Morton in 1931; this has relatively wide leaves but they are furnished on the margins with very conspicuous fleshy teeth. This occurs at the southern end of the range of *L. cotyledon* in the Trinity Alps region which is separated from the Siskiyou Mts. by the Klamath River basin. It was named after an Australian, J.H. Heckner, who was a Government Surveyor in Oregon. The material which later formed the type specimen was sent for identification to Ira Gabrielson who relayed it to the Smithsonian Institution in Washington where it was pronounced to be an undescribed species. Gabrielson wrote of Heckner that he was a 'keen-eyed woodsman who is very much interested in plants'.

Janet E. Hohn, in her Ph.D. thesis (1975), drew attention to another *L. cotyledon* variant occurring in Trinity County which also had undulate-margined leaves (actually described by her as 'fluted') and which she provisionally named subsp. *fimbriata*. I have not seen any living or dried examples of this so I am not in a position to comment about its validity as a distinct taxon. It was found in the Trinity River Gorge on vertical granite cliffs.

Other names which occur in literature in connection with *L. cotyledon* are *L. crenulata*, *L. longifolia*, *L. mariana* and *L. millardii*. These are all used by Samson Clay in *The Present Day Rock Garden* (1937) and are given a minimal description, insufficient to identify them with any degree of accuracy, and Clay himself expressed doubts about their authenticity. Since the International Rules of Nomenclature require that all descriptions published after 1935 should be in Latin, these names are in any case invalid.

Of all these named variants of *L. cotyledon* it seems that at least two are certainly worth recognizing at the rank of variety, var. *howellii* and the rather more distinct var. *heckneri*. However, it must be remembered that these taxa are variable and it appears that hybrids between them occur in the wild, and especially in gardens, so that individual plants may not be clearly identifiable with any of these varieties.

In addition to the above naturally occurring variants which have been given formal botanical names, others have been introduced to

117

cultivation and identified by means of cultivar names. For example, 'Kathy Kline' and 'Siskiyou White' are excellent pure albinos and 'Carroll Watson' is an unusual clear unstriped yellow which was found in the Rogue River Valley, Oregon. In gardens many different colour forms have been selected (PLATE 19B) and some of these have also received individual names such as 'Rose Splendour' (PLATE 11), an unstriped clear rose-pink from Mr A.G. Weeks of Limpsfield, Surrey. Mr Weeks was also the raiser of 'Weald Rose' which has particularly deep rich rosy purple flowers and narrow, rather crisped leaves indicating a connection with var. *howellii*. These named variants must be propagated vegetatively if they are to remain true to colour, since *L. cotyledon* usually varies enormously from seed and will hybridize with most other species if given the opportunity, although the hybrid offspring are usually sterile. Some nurserymen have raised large batches of seedlings and selected the best over a number of years; this has led to the marketing of excellent but variable groups such as the 'Sunset Strain' (PLATE 19A) from Jack Drake of Aviemore, Inverness-shire, and the 'Birch Hybrids' from W.E.Th. Ingwersen of East Grinstead, West Sussex. However, for all their splendid colours it seems that, judging from comments made by several field botanists, the horticultural selections of this species probably do not exceed the wild populations in their brilliance or range.

Lewisia cotyledon (S. Watson) B.L. Robinson in A. Gray, Syn. Fl. N. Amer. 1: 268 (1897). Type: N. California, Del Norte Co., 'near the head of Illinois River', June 1884, *Thomas Howell* (?GH).
Calandrinia cotyledon S. Watson in Proc. Amer. Acad. Arts 20: 355 (1885).
Oreobroma cotyledon (S. Watson) Howell in Erythea 1: 32 (1893).

DESCRIPTION. *Evergreen perennial* up to 30 cm in height when in flower, with the leaves forming tight flattish symmetrical rosettes up to 30 cm in diameter, but usually much less; sometimes multiple rosettes are formed, especially in cultivated plants; caudex short and thick, producing thick fleshy branching roots. *Basal leaves* deep green and slightly glaucous, sometimes tinged pinkish, spatulate, oblanceolate or obovate or sometimes almost linear or almost orbicular, 3–14 cm long, 10–40 mm wide, thick, fleshy, flat or slightly channelled on the upper surface, usually obtuse or rounded at the apex, narrowed at the base into a winged, keeled petiole; margin smooth, undulate, crisped, serrate at the apex or fimbriate-dentate.

Inflorescences consisting of fairly dense compact panicles, 10–30 cm in height. *Stem-leaves* alternate, oblong to ovate, 5–10 mm long, reduced and bract-like, glandular-dentate. *Bracts* obovate or lanceolate, 2–4 mm long, glandular-dentate. *Flowers* 2–4 cm in diameter. *Pedicels* short, 2–5 mm long. *Sepals* 2, suborbicular or broadly ovate, 4–6 mm long, 3.5–7 mm wide, obtuse to truncate at the apex, conspicuously veined, glandular-dentate. *Petals* 7–10, usually in some shade of pinkish purple with pale and dark stripes, but sometimes white, cream with pinkish orange stripes, apricot or yellow, oblanceolate, obovate or spatulate, (8–)10–20 mm long, 3–6 mm wide, rounded, obtuse, emarginate or dentate. *Stamens* 5–12. *Style* divided into 2–4 branches, sometimes very shortly so. *Capsule* narrowly oblong or ovoid, 3–5 mm long. *Seeds* 4–15, black, ovoid, *c.* 1.5 mm long, shiny.

Key to the Varieties of Lewisia cotyledon

1. Leaf-margins smooth, neither toothed nor crisped, sometimes slightly undulate; petals (8–)12–14 mm long .... a. var. **cotyledon**
   Leaf-margins toothed or markedly crisped-undulate; petals 12–20 mm long 2

2. Leaf-margins flat, furnished with conspicuous fleshy teeth; petals 16–20 mm long .... b. var. **heckneri**
   Leaf-margins strongly crisped-undulate; petals 12–15 mm long
   c. var. **howellii**

a. var. **cotyledon**

L. cotyledon var. *purdyi* Jepson, Fl. Calif. 5: 479 (1914). Type: Oregon, Josephine Co., Kirby, *C. Purdy* (?JEPS).

L. purdyi (Jepson) Gabrielson, West. Amer. Alpines 143, 144 (1932) in obs.

L. finchae Purdy in Leafl. W. Bot. 1: 20 (1932). Type: Oregon, Josephine Co., 'region around Waldo & Kirby', *Mrs J.M. Finch*, Herb. Cal. Acad. Sci. 193194 (CAS).

?*L. longifolia* S. Clay, Present Day Rock Garden xx, 341 (1937). No type designated, no Latin description.

ILLUSTRATIONS. PLATES 10, 19C. Curtis's Bot. Mag. 134: t.8220 (1908); R.C. Elliott, Lewisias (ed. 2) 21 (1978); Pacific Hort. 46(2): 45 (1985).

FLOWERING PERIOD. (May–)June–July.

HABITAT. Rock crevices in cliffs and paving in granite, serpentine, sandstone and schistose formations, usually on northern exposures, often with mosses; altitude 300–2290 m.

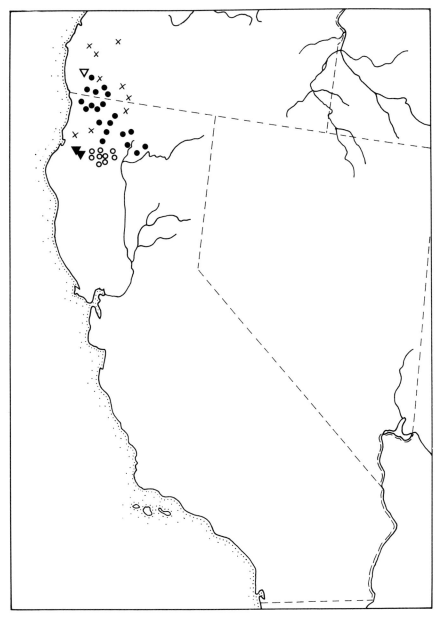

Map 15. Distribution of (●) *Lewisia cotyledon* var. *cotyledon*; (×) var. *howellii*; (○) var. *heckneri*. (▼) represents the variant provisionally known as 'fimbriata' (see p. 117). (▽) represents the variant known as var. *purdyi* (see p. 116).

120

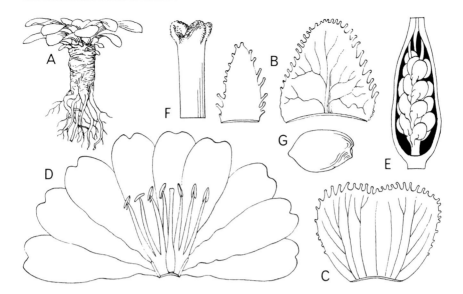

Lewisia cotyledon var. **cotyledon. A**, habit ×⅓; **B**, bracts, ×4; **C**, sepal, ×4; **D**, corolla, opened out, ×2; **E**, ovary with part of the wall removed, ×6; **F**, style-branches, ×12; **G**, seed, ×8.

DISTRIBUTION. USA: NW California (Klamath Ranges, Humboldt Co., Siskiyou Co., Del Norte Co. and Shasta Co.), SW Oregon (Josephine Co., Jackson Co. and Curry Co.). Records for Trinity Co., California probably all refer to var. *heckneri*. MAP 15, p. 120.

b. var. **heckneri** (C.V. Morton) Munz in Aliso 4: 90 (1958).
Oreobroma heckneri C.V. Morton in Proc. Biol. Soc. Wash. 44: 9 (1931).
   Type: California, Trinity Co., 4 mls N of Junction City near Canyon Creek, *J. Heckner*, U.S. Nat. Herb. 1439965 (US).
Lewisia heckneri (C.V. Morton) I.N. Gabrielson in New Fl. & Silva 5: 53 (1932).
?*L. mariana* S. Clay, Present Day Rock Garden xx, 341 (1937). No type designated, no Latin description.
?*L. millardii* S. Clay, Present Day Rock Garden xx, 341 (1937). No type designated, no Latin description.
   ILLUSTRATION. PLATE 11. R.C. Elliott, Lewisias (ed. 2) 22 (1978).
   FLOWERING PERIOD. May–July.
   HABITAT. Crevices and rocky slopes, usually on granite or basalt formations; altitude 450–2135 m.
   DISTRIBUTION. USA: N California (Trinity Co.). MAP 15, p. 120.

121

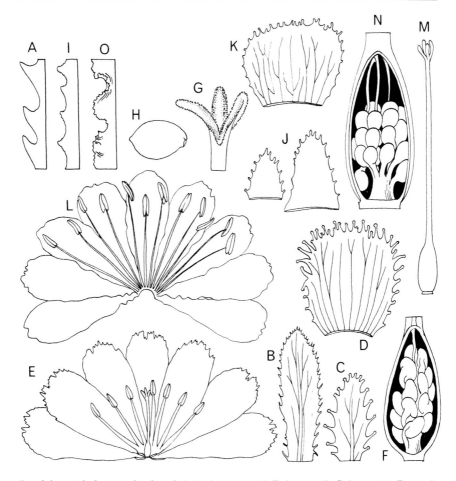

Lewisia cotyledon var. **heckneri. A**, leaf-margin, ×6; **B**, bract, ×2; **C**, bract, ×4; **D**, sepal, ×4; **E**, corolla, opened out, ×2; **F**, ovary with part of the wall removed, ×12; **G**, style-branches, ×12; **H**, seed, ×8. Var. **howellii. I**, leaf-margin, ×6; **J**, bracts, ×4; **K**, sepal, ×4; **L**, corolla, opened out, ×2; **M**, gynoecium, ×4; **N**, ovary with part of the wall removed, ×12. **Lewisia cotyledon** 'Rose Splendour'. **O**, leaf-margin, ×6.

c. var. **howellii** (S. Watson) Jepson, Fl. Calif. 5: 479 (1914).

Calandrinia howellii S. Watson in Proc. Amer. Acad. Arts 23: 262 (1888). Type: Oregon, Josephine Co., 'Deer Creek Mountains', July 1887, *T. Howell* 732 (?GH).

Oreobroma howellii (S. Watson) Howell in Erythea 1: 32 (1893).

Lewisia howellii (S. Watson) B.L. Robinson in A. Gray, Syn. Fl. N. Amer. 1: 268 (1897).

?L. crenulata S. Clay, Present Day Rock Garden xx, 341 (1937). No type designated, no Latin description.

ILLUSTRATION. PLATE 11. R.C. Elliott, Lewisias (ed. 2) 22 (1978).

FLOWERING PERIOD. April–May(–June).

HABITAT. Rock crevices and stony places, sometimes in open oak woodland; altitude 150–400 m.

DISTRIBUTION. USA: NW California (Humboldt Co. and Siskiyou Co.), SW Oregon (Curry Co., Josephine Co., Jackson Co. and ?Douglas Co.). MAP 15, p. 120.

19. LEWISIA TWEEDYI

To many gardeners *L. tweedyi* is the most glorious of its race and indeed is one of the most highly esteemed of all alpine plants. The very large flowers may lack the gaudy colours of *L. cotyledon* and its hybrids, but for some tastes they are much more attractive, in a quieter range of pastel shades of pinkish peach or yellowish apricot. It has been christened the 'Queen of lewisias' and is one of the gems of the flora of Washington State where it is known locally as the mountain rose and possibly also rock rose. As an ornamental plant its virtues were recognized early and it was cultivated as long ago as 1898 in the alpine house at the Royal Botanic Gardens, Kew, from a specimen purchased from the Columbia Nursery of Mr A.J. Johnson in Astoria, Oregon. It was illustrated for *Curtis's Botanical Magazine* (t.7633) in the following year and received an Award of Merit at a Royal Horticultural Society show in 1901 when exhibited by Messrs Barr of Covent Garden.

Lewisia tweedyi is, geographically speaking, a fairly restricted plant in the wild, occurring mainly in the Wenatchee range, an eastern spur of the great north-south Cascade mountain chain, although it is also recorded in the Cascades proper, northwards into southern British Columbia. It grows in rocky situations, often where there is a loose mixture of pine-needle duff (leaf-mould) and granite rock detritus, so the drainage is very sharp. The altitude range is considerable, from about 600 m up to more than 2000 m and Roy Davidson notes that at the higher altitudes it may occur on rock ledges as well as on the loose slopes, whereas lower down in the hotter canyons it is confined to the hillsides beneath pines. In the only locality where I have seen it, where it grows only a short distance from *L. rediviva*, it occurred on a very unstable slope in the

123

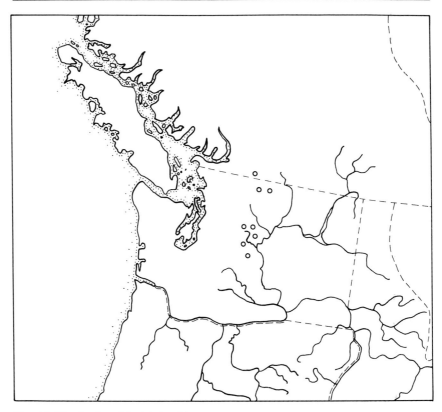

Map 16. Distribution of *Lewisia tweedyi*.

slight shade of pines, although some of the best plants were to be seen among small shrubs on the more stable rock outcrops. The plants are normally covered by snow in winter and must withstand considerable periods of heat and drought in summer, but they are able to cope with this by means of long fleshy roots which spread widely beneath the rocky surface. The nearby plants of *L. rediviva* were, by contrast, in full sun in very bare rocky situations which become baked in summer. The rainfall in the region is reported as being about 20 cm at Wenatchee but rising to 50 cm or more in the nearby mountains.

Lewisia tweedyi differs from all other species in its general appearance, with loose tufts of broadly obovate leaves just overtopped by very large pinkish flowers which may be 4–7 cm in diameter. It also differs in its seeds which are furnished at one end with a conspicuous

124

fleshy appendage, a pubescent scale-like structure, and in the surface architecture of the seed-coat which is also different from that of other species. It has been suggested that it might be better placed in another genus because of the seed characters, and by its apparent reluctance to hybridize with any other species. Certainly no proven hybrids of *L. tweedyi* have been seen, whereas it appears that nearly all the other species will cross readily between themselves when grown together. Some cytological studies in *Lewisia* have been undertaken and it is clear that in chromosome number *L. tweedyi* does differ (2n = 46 and 92 are recorded) from the other species, most of which have a diploid number of 2n = 28. It must be emphasized, however, that a thorough cytological survey of the genus has not been carried out and these observations are made only in order to give an indication that *L. tweedyi*, apart from its morpho-logical distinctness, does seem to be genetically in a class of its own with no near relatives. This lack of 'crossability' of *L. tweedyi* should not, however, necessarily be regarded as sufficient evidence for creating a separate genus for it and it would seem that on the basis of present evidence it is best retained in *Lewisia*. The seed characters, although obviously significant at specific level, may in fact not be of fundamental importance, for the surface architecture is just a more pronounced version of that seen on the testa of the seed of other species, while the fleshy appendage is apparently an outgrowth or extension of the pubescent scar which exists on the seeds of at least some of the other lewisias, if not all.

Lewisia tweedyi is, as indicated above, an excellent horticultural subject for the alpine enthusiast. Its appeal is enhanced by its ability to vary, particularly in flower colour, and this factor has led to a considerable amount of selecting of individual clones and strains, with colours ranging from pure clear pink to deep apricot and orange or yellow. Albinos have also been raised in cultivation, and found in the wild, and these are not all the same, some being pure white (PLATE 12) and others more ivory. A note by the well-known plantsman Roy Davidson of Seattle, taken from the *Bulletin of the Alpine Garden Club of British Columbia* for February 1973, is worth quoting for the observations on flower colour. 'In the wild this is almost invariably a lovely pastel peach colour, the result of a pink wash of pigmentation over a basic background of soft lemon-yellow; often this is variable in the same flower over its life span of a few days, usually deepening appreciably. Sometimes the blush is evident only concentrated on the margins, thus leaving a lemon or quite greenish star or eye effect in the centre of the blossom with the fluff of yellow stamens in its centre, but on occasion in wild plants the pink fails to develop, and the result is, of course, a fragile beauty in crisp lemony-citron, with yellow boss to match. Now, in cultivation, has emerged the other extreme, those with none of the minimum of the lemon yellow basic colour, so that the total effect is a pastel pink of great beauty.' Later, in 1983, Roy Davidson found a warm ivory-white form in the wild which he noted as being distinct from the pure white form cultivated and distributed by the Scottish nursery of Jack Drake which had originated in a batch of seed supplied by Charles Thurman of Spokane, Washington. This cultivar received an Award of Merit from the Royal Horticultural Society in 1978 as 'Alba'. Other named selections include a salmon-pink form (Neyron Rose HCC 623/1) called 'Rosea', which was awarded an Award of Merit on 14 April 1959, and 'Inshriach Strain' raised by Jack Drake and described as a slightly variable rich rose-red suffused with apricot.

Lewisia tweedyi was named after Frank Tweedy (1854–1937), a topographic engineer and amateur botanist who worked on the United States Geological Survey. It is, in the words of Roy Elliott (1966), 'probably the finest, the most popular (and certainly the most difficult in cultivation) of the entire genus'. Since that time, the cultivation needs of this lovely plant have become more fully understood and it is now considered to be relatively easy to keep for long periods: fine specimens may frequently be seen in the collections of alpine enthusiasts and botanic gardens.

Lewisia tweedyi (A. Gray) B.L. Robinson in A. Gray, Syn. Fl. N. Amer. 1: 268 (1897). Type: Washington, Wenatchee Mts., *Tweedy, Brandegee* (?GH).
Calandrinia tweedyi A. Gray in Proc. Amer. Acad. Arts 22: 277 (1887).
Oreobroma tweedyi (A. Gray) Howell in Erythea 1: 32 (1893).
L. aurantiaca A. Nelson in Univ. Wyoming Publ. Sci. Bot. 1: 62 (1924)
Type: Washington, Blewett Pass, 15 May 1922, *F. Bryant* in *E. Nelson* 1130 (location of specimen unknown).

DESCRIPTION. *Low, near-stemless, evergreen perennial* 10–20 cm in height at flowering time with loose tufts of basal leaves; caudex short with long thick fleshy roots, the caudex branching with age to produce several crowns. *Basal leaves* green, often with a purplish suffusion, broadly oblanceolate or obovate, 4–8 cm long, 25–50 mm wide, fleshy, entire, flat or slightly

Plate 19
A, *L. cotyledon* 'Sunset Strain' growing in a chimney-pot (photo. M. Ireland); **B**, *L. cotyledon* colour forms in cultivation (photo. M. Ireland); **C**, *L. cotyledon* var. *cotyledon*, Alex Hole, Siskiyou Co., California (photo. T. Walker).

Plate 20
A, *L. tweedyi*, Wenatchee Mts., Washington (photo. B. Mathew); **B**, *L. tweedyi*, location as A (photo. B. Mathew).

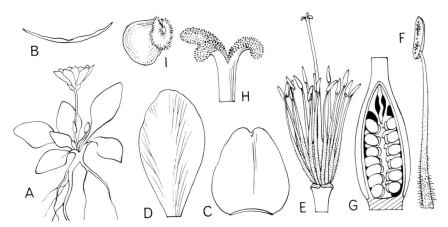

Lewisia tweedyi. A, habit (of a small specimen), ×⅓; **B**, leaf, transverse section, ×⅔; **C**, sepal, ×2; **D**, petal, ×1; **E**, gynoecium with stamens, ×2; **F**, stamen, ×4; **G**, ovary with part of the wall removed, ×6; **H**, style-branches, ×8; **I**, seed, ×6.

channelled, rounded, obtuse or emarginate at the apex, narrowed to a winged petiole 2–5 cm long, not forming a very symmetrical rosette. *Inflorescences* of several scapes, 10–20 cm long, each with 1–4(–8) flowers, usually leafless but sometimes with 1 or 2 reduced bract-like leaves near the base. *Bracts* alternate, broadly lanceolate, 5–10 mm long, scarious, entire, subtending the branches of the inflorescence. *Flowers* 4–5.5(–7) cm in diameter. *Pedicels* stout, fleshy, 2–6(–8.5) cm long. *Sepals* 2, broadly ovate, 9–10 mm long, rounded, obtuse or subacute, entire or minutely toothed, scarious, sometimes suffused purplish. *Petals* (7–)8–9(–12), pinkish peach to yellowish or rarely white, obovate, 2.5–4 cm long. *Stamens* 10–23. *Style* shortly divided into 3 branches. *Capsule* ovoid, somewhat 3-angled, 7–10 mm long. *Seeds* 12–30(–35), suborbicular-reniform, *c.* 2 mm long, conspicuously warted with a prominent scale-like, pubescent, deep brownish red or black fleshy appendage.

ILLUSTRATIONS. PLATE 12, 20A, B. Curtis's Bot. Mag. 125: t.7633 (1899); L.J. Clark, Wild Fl. Pacific Northwest 134 (1976); R.C. Elliott, Lewisias (ed. 2) 77 (1978); Pacific Hort. 46(2): 48, 49 (1985).

FLOWERING PERIOD. May–July.

HABITAT. Sharply drained rock (granitic) slopes or ledges, often in slight shade of *Pinus ponderosa* in light soil rich in humus ('pine duff'); altitude 600–2135 m.

DISTRIBUTION. USA: Washington State (southern Chelan Co. and northern Kittitas Co. in the Wenatchee Mts.). CANADA: British Columbia in the vicinity of Manning Park, and 'Walathian (Wallachian?) Mts.'. Probably also in other localities in the Cascade Mts. between these two areas. MAP 16, p. 124.

HYBRIDS

There appear to be few genetic barriers to hybridization in the genus *Lewisia*, except in the case of *L. tweedyi* which does not cross (at least, there are no authenticated cases of hybridization) with any other species. In their wild state not many of the species have the chance of hybridizing since they are separated geographically and perhaps, in some cases, by habitat as well. It is also possible that different pollinators are involved in certain instances but there is little available information about this.

These are physical barriers to hybridization, factors which cease to exist when the plants are brought into cultivation and, in the words of R.C. Elliott (1966), 'it simply is not possible to gather a selection of geographically separated species from different aspects, different soils and different altitudes, plant them side by side in lowland gardens on the other side of the Atlantic and expect them to behave with the restraint of a Papal Nuncio at a State Funeral'! In short, almost anything goes when the species of *Lewisia* are grown together in a situation where they can be cross-pollinated freely.

NATURALLY OCCURRING HYBRIDS

These appear to be rather rare, mainly for the reasons given above, that few of the species meet or overlap in their distributions in the wild, so the opportunity for liaisons does not often arise.

The only two crosses which have been reported, as far as I can trace, are:

1. **L. cotyledon** × **L. leeana** [Mrs Kath Dryden is of the opinion that *L. leeana* must be the seed parent; see p. 32)
   a. *L.* × *whiteae*. Described by Carl Purdy in *Leafl. W. Bot.* 1: 20 (1932) from a specimen collected by Mrs Mary L. White of Waldo, Oregon, deposited in the Herbarium of the California Academy of Sciences, no. 193196 (CAS). The locality is given

as Josephine County, Oregon, 'around Waldo'. It was described as having spatulate leaves 1 cm wide at the apex, and flowers with salmon-rose petals 12–13 mm long.

b. Roy Davidson (pers. comm.) tells me of a J.T. Howell specimen from Caribou Basin, Siskiyou County, California, 9 May 1932, which is apparently a hybrid with this parentage.

c. Recorded on Marble Mt., Siskiyou County, California. See Tucker, Mann & Holloway (1964). A plant from this collection subsequently received an Award of Merit in England, 18 April 1967, as *L.* 'Margaret Williams'.

d. Lawrence Crocker and Boyd Kline of the Siskiyou Rare Plant Nursery found a hybrid plant in the wild and it was introduced to cultivation as 'Timmie Foster'.

2. **L. nevadensis** × **L. triphylla**

a. A plant reported as a probable hybrid by Wayne Roderick at Castle Lake, Siskiyou County, California.

b. A single plant recorded by Gillett, Howell & Leschke (1961) in Lassen Volcanic National Park, California, is probably a hybrid between these two species.

ARTIFICIAL HYBRIDS

Unfortunately, most of the garden-raised hybrids in *Lewisia* appear to have arisen spontaneously and the parentage can only be guessed at. However, on the whole, the species have rather distinctive features so that if only two parents are involved the 'guesses' are likely to be fairly accurate. If, on the other hand, several species were involved in complex crosses it would almost certainly not be possible to work out the parentage of a particular plant. Most hybrids between distinct species are sterile so that the offspring do not progress beyond the first generation, other than by vegetative propagation. However, hybrids within a species, and one thinks particularly of the crosses between the varieties and other variants of *L. cotyledon*, are fertile, so that the process of hybridization and selection can be repeated over and over again to produce an everwidening range of variety. The excellent strains of *L. cotyledon* such as 'Sunset Strain' (Jack Drake) and 'Birch Hybrids' (W.E.Th. Ingwersen) are the results of such work.

The following list shows those species crosses which I have either seen as living plants or have located in the literature. In most cases it is not known which was the seed parent and which the pollen donor, so I have arranged them in alphabetical order.

A. **L. brachycalyx** × **L. cotyledon.** *Lewisia* 'Phyllellia' was raised by Joe Elliott in about 1950; this has the dwarf habit of *L. brachycalyx* but with pink flowers striped darker. Hybrids with this parentage have also been raised by Bob Putnam of Seattle and Fritz Kummert of Austria. Bedrich Parizek of Czechoslovakia has used *L. brachycalyx* as the female parent and obtained plants which, from the written description, appear to be similar to 'Phyllellia' but with flowers varying from rose-pink to yellow, presumably depending upon the flower colour of the *L. cotyledon* parent. The hybrids of this parentage are all evergreen although the leaf-rosettes look more like those of *L. brachycalyx*.

B. **L. brachycalyx** × **L. cotyledon** var. **heckneri.** Joe Elliott, about 1964, raised a hybrid which was named *L.* 'Brachyheck'.

C. **L. columbiana** × **L. cotyledon.** These two species cross fairly readily and have resulted in some aesthetically good plants which have persisted in cultivation. *Lewisia* 'Trevosia' originated as a self-sown seedling in the garden of Dr P.L. Guiseppi, Trevose, Felixstowe. It has become a well-known cultivar, almost certainly a cross between these two species, and received an Award of Merit on 25 May 1964. *Lewisia* 'George Henley' probably also has this parentage; this appeared in 1950 at the nursery of W.E.Th. Ingwersen, East Grinstead. It seems likely that *L. columbiana* is the seed parent of both of these cultivars.

B. Parizek of Czechoslovakia has made intentional crosses, both ways, using *L. cotyledon* and *L. columbiana* subsp. *rupicola*, and some of the plants are said to resemble 'George Henley'. When *L. cotyledon* was used as the female parent, the offspring were more vigorous than when *L. columbiana* was the seed parent.

D. **L. cantelovii** (♀) × **L. cotyledon.** Successful experimental crosses were carried out by Janet E. Hohn for a Ph.D. thesis (1975) at the University of Washington. Also *L. cantelovii* × *L. cotyledon* var. *heckneri*.

E. **L. cantelovii** (♀) × **L. leeana.** See note under D. above.

F. **L. cantelovii** (♀) × **L. columbiana.** See note under D. above.

130

G. **L. columbiana** subsp. **rupicola** × **L. rediviva** (♀). Reported by B. Parizek in *Bull. Amer. Rock Gard. Soc.* 1986: 196. Only one plant was obtained and this was evergreen with leaves about 2 mm wide (said to be *Armeria*-like) and had up to four violet flowers on short (2–5 cm) stalks.

H. **L. brachycalyx** × **L. sierrae** (♀). Two seedlings have been obtained by B. Parizek (see ref. in G. above). They are said to have flowers twice the size of *L. sierrae* and are very early flowering, earlier than either parent.

I. **L. cotyledon** × **L. longipetala** [almost certainly *L. longipetala* is the seed parent]. *Lewisia* 'Pinkie', which arose at the nursery of W.E.Th. Ingwersen Ltd., was originally thought to have been a *L. cotyledon* selection (*howellii* × *heckneri*). However, its features suggest that it is much more likely to be *L. cotyledon* × *L. longipetala* ('*pygmaea* of gardens'). This received an Award of Merit on 15 June 1965. Mrs Kath Dryden has noted that all the hybrids having *L. longipetala* as one of the parents have a strong musky or spicy fragrance, not just the flowers but the leaves and caudex also.

   Lewisia 'Oxstalls Lane' probably also has this parentage and is of similar habit and colour. *Lewisia* 'Matthew', raised by M. & R. Allen, of M & R Nurseries, is almost certainly also a *cotyledon* × *longipetala* cross with flowers of an orange shade.

   Lewisia 'Ben Chace' was a chance seedling at Ness Botanic Gardens and is considered to be a *L. cotyledon* × *L. pygmaea* (probably '*pygmaea* of gardens' = *L. longipetala*) cross. See P. Cunnington, in the *Bulletin of the Alpine Garden Society* 53: 12 (1985).

J. **L. cotyledon** × **L. oppositifolia** [it is fairly certain that *L. oppositifolia* is the seed parent]. This was a cross made in 1921 by Mr Gosden, reported in the *Journal of the Royal Horticultural Society* 48: lxxii (1923); it received a Botanical Certificate when shown to the Scientific Committee on 9 August 1922. Like *L. oppositifolia* it was a deciduous plant but had orange flowers, veined with pink.

K. **L. cotyledon** × **L. rediviva.** This cross was first made in the 1960s by Joe Elliott who called his plants *L.* 'Redicot'. It has also been made by Fritz Kummert in Austria and by B. Parizek in Czechoslovakia. The results appear to be very variable, largely due no doubt to the fact that both parents are variable. Some crosses are noted as being more like *L. rediviva* in habit and leaf shape (although evergreen) while others have leaf-rosettes more like *L. cotyledon* but with narrower leaves. The flowers usually seem to be pink or yellowish with darker stripes, more like *L. cotyledon* in colour but in their large size showing some of the influence of *L. rediviva*. The hybrids have nearly all had *L. rediviva* as the female parent but B. Parizek has also tried the cross with *L. cotyledon* as the seed parent, resulting in plants which have evergreen rosettes of narrow leaves and 10 cm stalks bearing flowers which are only slightly larger than those of *L. cotyledon*. *Lewisia* 'Pam', raised by Dr John Good, about 1977, is reputedly a *rediviva* × *cotyledon* hybrid, and *Lewisia* 'Rawreth' is another cultivar having this parentage, raised by D. Mann.

L. **L. cotyledon** var. **howellii** × **L. rediviva.** *Lewisia* 'Weeks' Seedling' was reputed to have this parentage, and the photograph in the *Bulletin of the Alpine Garden Society* 15: 216 (1947) appears to support this. It received an Award of Merit on 1 July 1947.

M. **L. longipetala** × **L. rediviva.** A plant seen by me at the Royal Botanic Gardens, Kew in 1987 clearly has this parentage. This came from Mrs Kath Dryden who tells me that hybrid plants started appearing spontaneously in her collection of lewisias, and so she then undertook some intentional hybridizing. The best of the seedlings was a pink-flowered one and was called 'Roy Elliott'; other good ones have been named 'Andrew' and 'Christine', both with pure white flowers. At Kew, Tony Hall has also recently raised a hybrid which clearly has this parentage.

This is by no means a complete list of all the hybrids which have been produced artificially. Mrs. Kath Dryden, for instance, records that *L. brachycalyx* will cross with *L. longipetala*, *L. oppositifolia* and *L. rediviva*, in addition to all those crosses already mentioned above. Doubtless many other combinations of species are possible.

CULTIVARS

As mentioned previously, some of the cultivars are the result of hybridization between species, while others have arisen through a process of selection within a species. The following alphabetical list of cultivar (and a few hybrid Latinized) names is a selection of some of the better known or currently available ones to be found in cultivation, and in catalogues and other literature.

'Alba'. An albino *L. cotyledon*. See notes under 'Kathy Kline' below.

'Ashwood Pearl'. Raised by Philip Baulk of Ashwood Nurseries, Kingswinford, W Midlands. A compact semi-deciduous plant with narrow leaves and pearl-white flowers. A *L. longipetala* × *L. cotyledon* cross.

'Ashwood Strain'. A variable strain of *L. cotyledon* in a wide range of mixed colours. Ashwood Nurseries.

'Ashwood Yellows'. A *L. cotyledon* strain in the yellow shades, ranging from lemon-yellow to gold. The cultivar 'Harold Judd' was used as the starting point for this strain. Ashwood Nurseries.

'Ben Chace'. A self-sown seedling at the University of Liverpool's Botanic Garden, Ness, in 1975. Said to be *L. cotyledon* × *L. pygmaea* but probably *L. cotyledon* × *L. longipetala*. It has evergreen leaf-rosettes with narrow leaves and short inflorescences bearing clear, pale pink flowers about 3 cm in diameter. It has a spicy fragrance (see note under 'Pinkie', below).

'Brachyheck' (or × *brachyheck*). Raised by Joe Elliott of Moreton-in-Marsh, Gloucestershire in about 1964; a cross between *L. brachycalyx* and *L. cotyledon* var. *heckneri*. It is a dwarf evergreen plant with short-stemmed white or pink flowers resting amid the leaves.

'Carroll Watson'. A pale clear unstriped yellow *L. cotyledon* variant found in 1969 at 600 m in the Siskiyou Mts., California by Mr

Watson, and named after his daughter. Award of Merit 24 May 1974.

'**Comet**'. A *L. cotyledon* selection. Exhibited 3 June 1960 at a show in Dunfermline by Messrs Jack Drake.

'**Edithae**' (or × *edithae*). Raised by Carl S. English, a cross between *L. columbiana* and *L. columbiana* subsp. *rupicola*. It is a free-flowering vigorous plant which produces small, stalked rosettes which may be detached for vegetative propagation as cuttings.

'**George Henley**'. A *L. columbiana* × *L. cotyledon* hybrid, raised in about 1958 in the nursery of W.E.Th. Ingwersen Ltd. and named after the nursery manager. It is a compact plant (about 15 cm in height) with wine-red flowers 2 cm in diameter. Received an Award of Merit 22 May 1978. See colour illustration in *Bulletin of the Alpine Garden Society* 55: 38 (1987).

'**Golden West**'. A *L. cotyledon* selection. Exhibited by Messrs Jack Drake at a show in Dunfermline on 3 June 1960.

'**Harold Judd**'. A *L. cotyledon* selection which is compact in growth with clear yellow flowers. It has been used by Ashwood Nurseries in a breeding programme to produce a wide colour range, including the 'Ashwood Yellows' strain. It was selected from a batch of seedlings grown by Byatt's nursery in Hampton in the late 1950s or early 1960s.

'**Jean Turner**'. Probably a *L. cotyledon* selection, raised by J.B. Turner of Birmingham from a packet of seed from the Alpine Garden Society's distribution of 1957. It had large pink flowers and a vigorous constitution. Illustrated in R.C. Elliott, *Lewisias* (ed. 2) 71 (1978).

'**Jennifer**'. A *L. cotyledon* selection raised from a var. *cotyledon* × var. *howellii* cross by Royton E. Heath. Exhibited at a Royal Horticultural Society show on 23 May 1951.

'**Jolon**'. A variant of *L. rediviva* introduced by Wayne Roderick from Jolon, California. It has very large mid-pink flowers (RHS Red Group 55C). The flowers of the offspring have been found to vary from white to pink. It was given an Award of Merit when exhibited by Mrs Kath Dryden on 24 May 1976.

'Kathy Kline'. An albino *L. cotyledon*, the confused history of which (and its offspring) has been related to me by Kath Dryden. It originated as a single plant found in the Siskiyou Mountains by Marcel Le Piniec of Oregon, and was introduced into cultivation. Unlike most *L. cotyledon* forms in the wild, it produced many side rosettes, so a vegetatively propagated stock was built up in the Siskiyou Rare Plant Nursery of Lawrence Crocker and Boyd Kline, and was distributed from there. In order to exhibit the plant Kath Dryden requested a cultivar name from Boyd Kline, who suggested 'Kathy Kline', under which name it received a First Class Certificate on 22 May 1972. Seeds were also collected from the plant and distributed by the Siskiyou nursery, and from these other white-flowered cultivars were raised and given names such as 'Siskiyou White', 'Alba' and 'Monsieur Le Piniec'. The last two received a joint Award of Merit on 12 May 1972 and were subsequently bracketed together as forma *alba* by R. Gorer in *Bulletin of the Alpine Garden Society* 40: 319 (1972), a name which will now suffice for any albino *L. cotyledon*.

Mrs Kath Dryden notes that 'Kathy Kline' is distinct from other albinos in that it produces side rosettes, so that it can be increased by cuttings and maintained as a clone. It is a fine plant, very floriferous with large white flowers and has smooth leaves (not toothed or wavy), rather pale and almost rounded. Seeds from it produce about 95 per cent white-flowered seedlings but these should not be called 'Kathy Kline', just forma *alba*.

To be really accurate the full name of the cultivar should be *L. cotyledon* var. *cotyledon* forma *alba* 'Kathy Kline'!

'Kline's Red'. A *L. cotyledon* selection with rich reddish purple flowers, introduced by Boyd Kline.

'Late Orange'. An orange-flowered *L. cotyledon* selection. Catalogued by W.E.Th. Ingwersen Ltd. in 1982.

'Margaret Williams'. A *L. leeana* × *L. cotyledon* hybrid found by Dr J.M. Tucker in the Marble Mts. south of the Siskiyou Range where the two species grow together (see Tucker, Mann & Holloway, 1964). It was introduced into cultivation and given the cultivar name under which it received an Award of Merit on 18 April 1967. It has narrow leaves and a rosette shape which tends towards *L. leeana* but the flowers show characteristics of *L. cotyledon*; they are a dark cerise-red in colour.

Another hybrid with this parentage was found in the wild by Lawrence Crocker and Boyd Kline of the Siskiyou Rare Plant Nursery, Oregon. This was also brought into cultivation, as 'Timmie Foster', but Mrs Kath Dryden reports that attempts to introduce and grow it in Britain have so far failed. It has pale cream flowers with a rose-pink centre. Kath Dryden is of the opinion that of the *leeana* × *cotyledon* hybrids, it is the former which is the seed parent (see p. 32).

'Matthew'. A *L. longipetala* × *L. cotyledon* hybrid with the general habit of the well-known 'Pinkie' (see below) but with creamy yellowish orange flowers. Raised by M. & R. Allen of M & R Nurseries.

'Monsieur Le Piniec'. An albino *L. cotyledon*. See notes under 'Kathy Kline' above.

'Oxstalls Lane'. Probably a *L. longipetala* × *L. cotyledon* hybrid, similar in overall appearance to the well-known 'Pinkie' (see below). The flowers are pink with deep red stamens (anthers).

'Pam'. *L. rediviva* (♀) × (probably) *L. cotyledon*. Raised by Dr John Good, about 1977. It has neat rosettes and 5 cm stems carrying large flowers of an unusual shade of pink flushed with cerise.

'Paula'. A *L. cotyledon* selection (or hybrid?) with pale purple flowers, raised by W.E.Th. Ingwersen Ltd. (?1970s) and named after Paula Ingwersen.

'Phyllellia'. A *L. brachycalyx* × *L. cotyledon* hybrid, raised by Joe Elliott of Broadwell Nursery, Moreton-in-Marsh, Gloucestershire, in the 1940s or early 1950s. It has the compact habit of *L. brachycalyx* but the flowers are rather like those of *L. cotyledon*, pale pink and striped darker. Received a Preliminary Commendation on 24 April 1951 and an Award of Merit on 12 May 1972. Alternative spellings found in literature are 'Phylellia' and 'Phyllelia'.

'Pinkie'. A *L. longipetala* × *L. cotyledon* hybrid, raised by W.E.Th. Ingwersen in the ?1960s. It has compact flattish evergreen rosettes of narrow leaves and stems *c.* 10 cm tall carrying flowers 2–2.5 cm in diameter, of a pale pink shade (HCC Persian Rose 628/2–628/3) with yellow in the centre; the calyx has conspicuous crimson glandular teeth. Kath Dryden has noted that all the *L. longipetala* hybrids have a musky or spicy smell, not just the flowers but all parts of the plant. Received an Award of Merit on 15 June 1965. See illustration in R.C. Elliott, *Lewisias* (ed. 2) 70 (1978).

'Rawreth'. This was raised by the wholesale nurseryman Mr Don Mann and named by Mrs Kath Dryden. The seed parent was *L. rediviva* and the pollen parent is assumed to be *L. cotyledon* 'Rose Splendour'. It is almost deciduous with leaves and habit like those of *L. rediviva* but has flowers similar to 'Rose Splendour', but on stems only 5 cm long.

'Rose Splendour'. PLATE 11. A selection of *L. cotyledon* var. *howellii* raised in the 1940s or early 1950s by Mr A.G. Weeks of Limpsfield Chart, Surrey. The flowers are a clear strong rose, not conspicuously striped (HCC Mallow Purple 630/1 shading to 630/3). Received an Award of Merit on 4 May 1965.

'Roy Elliott'. Raised by Mrs Kath Dryden. It is a hybrid between *L. longipetala* and *L. rediviva* 'Jolon', selected as being the best of the pink seedlings and described by her as being 'icing sugar pink'.

'Siskiyou Champagne'. A strain of *L. rediviva* raised by Mrs Kath Dryden from a white *L. rediviva*. Its champagne-coloured flowers have many narrow petals and pink anthers.

'Siskiyou White'. An albino *L. cotyledon*. See notes under 'Kathy Kline' above.

'Sunset Strain'. PLATE 19A. A variable brightly coloured strain of *L. cotyledon* raised by Messrs Jack Drake of Inshriach Nursery, Aviemore, Inverness-shire.

'Susan'. A *L. cotyledon* selection (or hybrid?) with rose-purple flowers, raised by W.E.Th. Ingwersen Ltd. (?1970s) and named after Susan Ingwersen.

'Timmie Foster'. See notes under 'Margaret Williams' and × *whiteae*.

'Trevosia'. A *L. columbiana* × *L. cotyledon* (var. *howellii*) hybrid which arose as a self-sown seedling in the alpine house of Dr P.L. Guiseppi of Trevose, Felixstowe, in the 1940s. It has the general appearance of *L. columbiana* with narrow leaves (5–10 mm wide) and has tall slender stems carrying flowers 2 cm in diameter, pinkish orange with pinkish purple centres (HCC Rose Opal 022/2 at first, shading to Persian Rose 628/2). Received a Preliminary Commendation on 20 May 1947, and an Award of Merit on 25 May 1964. Illustrated in R.C. Elliott, *Lewisias* (ed. 2) 72 (1978).

'Weald Gold'. A golden-coloured *L. cotyledon* selection, raised by Mr A.G. Weeks of Weald Cottage, Limpsfield Chart, Surrey. Exhibited on 18 April 1961.

'Weald Rose'. A selection of *L. cotyledon* var. *howellii*, raised in 1948 by Mr A.G. Weeks of Limpsfield Chart, Surrey and named after his house, Weald Cottage. It is a compact plant, about 15 cm in height, with rosettes of crisped-margined leaves and strong reddish flowers (HCC Spiraea Red 025/1) with paler and darker suffusion. Received an Award of Merit on 23 May 1951.

'Weeks' Seedling'. Probably a *L. cotyledon* var. *howellii* × *L. rediviva* hybrid, raised by Mr A.G. Weeks of Limpsfield Chart, Surrey, in the 1940s. It had compact stems bearing large (3.5–4 cm in diameter) flowers, pale pink with darker veins. It received an Award of Merit on 1 July 1947 and is illustrated in *Bulletin of the Alpine Garden Society* 15: 216 (1947).

× **whiteae.** A natural hybrid between *L. cotyledon* and *L. leeana*. Mrs Kath Dryden is of the opinion that the latter is the seed parent (see p. 32). Collected in the Siskiyou Mts. by Mrs Mary L. White of Waldo, and described as a species by Carl Purdy in *Leafl. W. Bot.* 1: 20 (1932). It has rather narrow leaves and salmon-rose flowers and is still in cultivation from this original collection. Since the name *whiteae* is, botanically-speaking, validly published it can be used for any *L. cotyledon*—*L. leeana* hybrid, in which case the individual collected by Mrs White, and its vegetatively produced offspring, should be given a cultivar name such as *L.* × *whiteae* 'Mary White', a suggestion made to me by Roy Davidson of Seattle. Another hybrid was found by Lawrence Crocker and Boyd Kline of the Siskiyou Rare Plant Nursery, with pale cream rose-centred flowers; this was named 'Timmie Foster'. The cultivar 'Margaret Williams' (above) should correctly be referred to as *L.* × *whiteae* 'Margaret Williams'.

'Winifred Herdman'. A *L. rediviva* variant which is thought to have come from the Okanagan Valley in British Columbia. The flowers are soft pink and about 7.5 cm across. Award of Merit 24 May 1927.

APPENDIX 1
New Taxa

Subgen. **Lewisia**
Semina non-tuberculata, estrophiolata.
Type of subgenus: *L. rediviva* Pursh

Sect. **Lewisia**
Plantae deciduae; pedicelli articulati, floribus totis in statu fructifero delapsis; sepala 2–9, scariosa.
Type of section: *L. rediviva* Pursh

Sect. **Brachycalyx** B. Mathew, **sect. nov.**
Plantae deciduae; inflorescentia uniflora; flores sessiles, bracteis sepala contingentibus.
Type of section: *L. brachycalyx* Engelm. ex A. Gray

Sect. **Erocallis** B. Mathew, **sect. nov.**
Plantae deciduae, unaquaque tubere globoso oriens; folia caulina bene evoluta, plerumque terna in verticillo disposita.
Type of section: *L. triphylla* (S. Watson) B.L. Robinson

Sect. **Oppositifolia** B. Mathew, **sect. nov.**
Plantae deciduae; folia caulina bene evoluta, binata; pedicelli longi, tenues.
Type of section: *L. oppositifolia* (S. Watson) B.L. Robinson

Sect. **Pygmaea** B. Mathew, **sect. nov.**
Plantae deciduae; inflorescentia uniflora vel pauciramulosa; folia plerumque aliquantum angusta.
Type of section: *L. pygmaea* (A. Gray) B.L. Robinson

Sect. **Cotyledon** J.E. Hohn ex B. Mathew, **sect. nov.**
Plantae plerumque semperviventes; inflorescentiae elatae, ramosissimae; folia plerumque aliquantum lata.
Type of section: *L. cotyledon* (S. Watson) B.L. Robinson

Subgen. **Strophiolum** (J.E. Hohn) ex B. Mathew, **subgen. nov.**
Semina tuberculata, strophiolo carnoso prominenti instructa.
Type of subgenus: *L. tweedyi* (A. Gray) B.L. Robinson

APPENDIX 2
Dates of publication of *Lewisia* species and dates of introduction into cultivation in Britain

The following list of species is arranged in chronological order of the date of first publication. Most *Lewisia* species were first described in other genera such as *Talinum*, *Calandrinia*, *Oreobroma*, etc. The dates of introduction are approximations and in some cases the actual dates may be somewhat earlier than the estimated ones given.

L. rediviva — Pursh (1814).   Cultivated Royal Botanic Gardens, Kew 1863.

L. pygmaea — A. Gray (1862) as *Talinum*.   Cultivated Bees of Neston 1907.

L. brachycalyx — Engelm. ex A. Gray (1868).   Cultivated Royal Botanic Gardens, Kew 1875.

L. nevadensis — A. Gray (1873) as *Calandrinia*.   Cultivated 1880.

L. triphylla — S. Watson (1875) as *Claytonia*.   Rarely cultivated in Britain.

L. leeana — T. Porter (1876) as *Calandrinia*.   Cultivated Bulley, Neston *c.* 1903.

L. oppositifolia — S. Watson (1885) as *Calandrinia*.   Cultivated Royal Botanic Gardens, Kew 1888.

L. cotyledon — S. Watson (1885) as *Calandrinia*.   Cultivated Royal Botanic Gardens, Kew 1906.

L. tweedyi — A. Gray (1887) as *Calandrinia*.   Cultivated Royal Botanic Gardens, Kew 1898.

L. columbiana — Howell ex A. Gray (1887) as *Calandrinia*.   Cultivated Bulley, Neston before 1907.

L. kelloggii — K. Brandegee (1894).   Perhaps never successfully cultivated in Britain.

L. longipetala — Piper (1913) as *Oreobroma*.   Probably cultivated in Britain since at least 1950s as *L. pygmaea*.

L. congdonii — Rydberg (1932) as *Oreobroma*.   Probably introduced to Britain in 1970s.

140

L. disepala—Rydberg (1932). *L. disepala* was known long before this, as *L. rediviva* var. *yosemitana* K. Brandegee (1894).

Perhaps never successfully cultivated in Britain.

L. cantelovii—J.T. Howell (1942).

Recorded in cultivation in Britain in 1971.

L. sierrae—Ferris (1944).

Cultivated since 1970s in Britain.

L. maguirei—A.H. Holmgren (1954).

Perhaps never successfully cultivated in Britain.

L. stebbinsii—Gankin & Hildreth (1968).

Recorded in cultivation in Britain in 1979.

L. serrata—Heckard & Stebbins (1974).

Cultivated in Britain since 1970s.

APPENDIX 3
Royal Horticultural Society Awards to lewisias

Preliminary Commendation (P.C.), First Class Certificate (F.C.C.) or Award of Merit (A.M.).

The list of species and their variants is given in alphabetical order, followed by a list of awards to hybrid cultivars. In some instances the names under which the plants received their awards are synonyms; in these cases the correct names are given, followed by the award names in square brackets. P.C.s are not included if the plants have subsequently been given an A.M. or F.C.C.

L. brachycalyx	A.M.	3 May 1938 (Mrs A.N. Griffith)
L. columbiana	A.M.	18 May 1915 (Miss E. Willmott)
L. cotyledon	A.M.	23 May 1911 (G. Reuthe)
L. cotyledon forma *alba* 'Kathy Kline'	F.C.C.	22 May 1972 (Mrs K.N. Dryden)
L. cotyledon forma *alba* 'Monsieur Le Piniec'	A.M.	12 May 1972 (Mrs E. Ivey & H. Esslemont)
L. cotyledon forma *heckneri* [as *L. heckneri*]	A.M.	24 May 1932 (Sir W. Lawrence)
L. cotyledon forma *howellii* [as *L. howellii*]	A.M.	30 April 1912 (M. Prichard)
L. cotyledon 'Carroll Watson'	A.M.	24 May 1974 (J.D. Crosland)
L. cotyledon 'Rose Splendour'	A.M.	4 May 1965 (W.E.Th. Ingwersen)
L. cotyledon 'Weald Rose'	A.M.	23 May 1951 (A.G. Weeks)
L. oppositifolia	A.M.	19 May 1970 (Mrs K.N. Dryden)
L. oppositifolia 'Richeyi' [as *L. richeyi*]	P.C.	18 June 1935 (G.P. Baker)
L. pygmaea	A.M.	11 June 1929 (RHS, Wisley)
L. rediviva	F.C.C.	1873 (Backhouse)
L. rediviva 'Jolon'	A.M.	24 May 1976 (Mrs K.N. Dryden)
L. rediviva 'Winifred Herdman'	A.M.	24 May 1927 (C. van Tubergen)
L. tweedyi	A.M.	4 June 1901 (Messrs Barr)

L. tweedyi 'Alba'	A.M.	18 April 1978 (Mrs J. Bishop)
L. tweedyi 'Rosea'	A.M.	14 April 1959 (W.E.Th. Ingwersen)

Hybrid cultivars. Known or supposed parentage is shown in brackets.

'George Henley'
    (*L. columbiana* × ?*L. cotyledon*)   A.M.   22 May 1978 (W.E.Th. Ingwersen)

'Margaret Williams'
    (*L. leeana* × *L. cotyledon*)   A.M.   18 April 1967 (Mrs K.N. Dryden)

'Phyllellia'
    (*L. brachycalyx* × *L. cotyledon*)   A.M.   12 May 1972 (Mrs E. Ivey)

'Pinkie'
    (?*L. cotyledon* × *L. longipetala*)   A.M.   15 June 1965 (W.E.Th. Ingwersen)

'Trevosia'
    (*L. columbiana* × *L. cotyledon*)   A.M.   25 May 1964 (Joe Elliott)

'Weeks' Seedling'
    (*L. cotyledon* × *L. rediviva*)   A.M.   1 July 1947

BIBLIOGRAPHY

Baker, G. (1987). Plant Portraits—Lewisia cotyledon. *The Rock Garden* (*J. Scot. Rock Gard. Club*) 20: 233–4.

Baulk, P. (1988a). *Lewisias, A cultural guide*. Ashford Nurseries publication, Kingswinford, W Midlands, UK.

—— (1988b). My Lewisia Year. *Bull. Alpine Gard. Soc.* 56: 243–51.

Bentham, G. & Hooker, J.D. (1862). *Genera Plantarum* 1: 155–9.

Brandegee, K. (1894). Studies in Portulacaceae. *Proc. Calif. Acad. Sci.*, ser. 2(4): 86–91.

Clay, S. (1937). Lewisia. In *The Present Day Rock Garden* 340–2.

Colley, J. Cobb & Mineo, B. (1985). Lewisias for the garden. *Pacific Hort.* 46: 40–9.

Coues, E. (1899). Notes on Mr Thomas Meehan's paper on the plants of the Lewis and Clark's expedition across the continent. *Acad. Nat. Sci. Philadelphia* 1898: 291–315.

Daubenmire, R. (1975). An ecological life history of Lewisia rediviva (Portulacaceae). *Syesis* 8: 9–23 (1975).

Elliott, R.C. (1966). The Genus Lewisia. *Bull. Alpine Gard. Soc.* 34: 1–76. Also issued as a separate booklet, *Lewisias*, in 1966; Ed. 2 (1978).

—— (1979). The Lewisia story. *Plantsman* 1: 5–11.

Engler, A. (1964). *Syllabus der Pflanzenfamilien* (ed. 12) 2: 79.

Fenzl, E. (1836). Monographie der Mollugineen und Steudelieen. *Ann. Wiener Mus. Naturgesch.* 1: 337–84.

—— (1839). Supplement. Verbesserungen und Züsatze zur ersten Abteilung der Monographie in *Ann. Wiener Mus. Naturgesch.* 2: 279–307.

Ferris, R.S. in Abrams, L. (1944). Portulacaceae. *Ill. Flora Pacific States* 2: 131.

Gabrielson, I.N. (1932). Lewisia, in *Western American Alpines* 141–7.

Gankin, R. & Hildreth, W.R. (1968). A new species of Lewisia from Mendocino County, California. *Four Seasons* 2: 12–14.

Gillett, G.W., Howell, J.T. & Leschke, H. (1961). A Flora of Lassen Volcanic National Park, California. *Wasmann Journ. Biol.* 19: 1–185.

Gray, A. (1886). Contributions to American Botany I. Revision of some polypetalous genera and orders precursory to the Flora of North America. *Proc. Amer. Acad. Arts* 22: 270–306.

Harrington, H.D. (1954). Portulacaceae. In *Manual of the Plants of Colorado* 223–5.

Hart, J. (1976). Bitterroot, Lewisia rediviva Pursh. *Montana — Native Plants and Early People* 46–9.

Heckard, L.R. & Stebbins, G.L. (1974). A new Lewisia (Portulacaceae) from the Sierra Nevada of California. *Brittonia* 26: 305–8.

Hitchcock, C.L. *et al.* (1964). Portulacaceae. In *Vascular plants of the Pacific Northwest* 2: 225–49.

Hohn, J.E. (1975). Biosystematic studies of the genus Lewisia, section Cotyledon (Portulacaceae). Unpublished PhD thesis, University of Washington.

Holmgren, A.H. (1955). Portulacaceae of Nevada. *Contr. towards a Flora of Nevada* No. 36: 1–18.

Hooker, W.J. & Arnott, G. (1839). Lewisiaceae. *Bot. Beech.* 344, t. 86 (1839).

Howell, T. (1893). A rearrangement of American Portulaceae. *Erythea* 1: 29–41.

Hutchinson, J. (1973). *The families of Flowering Plants* (ed. 3) 533.

Jepson, W.L. (1914). Portulacaceae. In *A Flora of California* 1: 463–80.

Kearney, T.H. & Peebles, R.H. (1951). Portulacaceae. In *Arizona Flora* 285–91.

Kelley, W.A. & Swanson, J.R. (1985). Oreobroma megarhizum is a Calandrinia of section Acaules (Portulacaceae). *Brittonia* 37(1): 56–7.

Kruckeberg, A.R. (1957). Documented chromosome numbers of plants. *Madroño* 14: 111–12.

Lowzow, S. (1986). Lewisia brachycalyx in cultivation. *Bull. Canterbury Alp. Gard. Soc.* 1986: 54.

MacBryde, B. (1973). A Lewisia native to Mexico and Guatemala. *J. Scot. Rock Gard. Club* 13: 294–6.

McNeill, J. (1973). Lewisia triphylla . . ., new species for Canada. *Syesis* 6: 179–81.

—— (1974). Synopsis of a revised classification of the Portulacaceae. *Taxon* 23: 725–8.

Martin, W.C. & Hutchins, C.R. (1980). Portulacaceae. In *A Flora of New Mexico* 1: 679–90.

Millard, F.W. (1935). Lewisias at Camla. *J. Roy. Hort. Soc.* 60: 159–61.

Munz, P.A. (1959). Portulacaceae. In *A California Flora*: 295–306.

—— (1963). Lewisia. *California Mountain Wildflowers* 15, 30.

Newcomer, E.J. (1933). Lewisias in their native home. *Nat. Hort. Mag.* 12: 58–61.

Parizek, B. (1986). Some experience in breeding Lewisias. *Bull. Amer. Rock Gard. Soc.* 193–6.

Pax, F. & Hoffmann, K. (1934). Portulacaceae. In Engler, A. & Harms, H. *Die Natürlichen Pflanzenfamilien* (ed. 2), 16c: 234–62.

Peck, M.E. (1941). Portulacaceae. In *A Manual of the Higher Plants of Oregon* 274–82.

Piper, C.V. (1906). Portulacaceae. In *Flora of the State of Washington* 245–51.

Pursh, F. (1814). Lewisia. In *Flora Americae Septentrionalis* 2: 368.

Robinson, B.L. (1897). Lewisia. In Gray, A. *et al.*, *Synoptical Flora of North America* 1: 266–9.

Rowntree, L. (1972). *Bull. Alpine Gard. Soc.* 40: 10.

Rudd, V.E. (1954). Botanical contributions of the Lewis and Clark Expedition. *Journ. Washington Acad. Sci.* 44: 351–6.

Rydberg, P.A. (1906). Portulacaceae. In *Flora of Colorado* 125–6.

—— (1918). Lewisia. In *Flora of the Rocky Mountains and Adjacent Plains* 262–6.

—— (1932). Portulacaceae. In *North Amer. Flora* 21: 279–336.

St John, H. (1929). New and noteworthy northwestern plants. *Res. Stud. State Coll. of Wash.* 1(1): 59–62.

Tidestrom, I. (1925). Portulacaceae. In *Flora of Utah and Nevada* 185–9.

Torrey, J. & Gray, A. (1840). Portulacaceae. In *A Flora of North America* 1: 677–8.

Tucker, J.M., Mann, L.K. & Holloway, S.L. (1964). A natural hybrid in the genus Lewisia. *Cactus & Succulent Journal* 36: 47–50.

Walker, S. (1986). Lewisia brachycalyx in the wild. *Bull. Canterbury Alp. Gard. Soc.* 53.

Welsh, S.L. *et al.* (1987). Portulacaceae. In *A Utah Flora* 493–7.

Wiens, D. & Halleck, D.K. (1962). Chromosome numbers in Rocky Mountain plants. *Bot. Notiser* 115: 455–64.

INDEX TO SPECIFIC AND INFRASPECIFIC EPITHETS

Accepted names are given in roman type; synonyms are in *italic* type.